THE ECLOGUES AND GEORGICS OF VIRGIL

C. DAY LEWIS was born in England and educated at Sherborne School and Wadham College, Oxford. In the course of an extended teaching career, he has been a Clark Lecturer at Trinity College, Cambridge, and Professor of Poetry at Oxford University from 1951–56. During 1958 he served as Vice-President of the Royal Society of Literature.

Mr. Day Lewis has published several novels as well as many volumes of poetry, including *Collected Poems, 1954, A Time to Dance, Overtures to Death, Poems in Wartime, Word Over All, Poems, 1943–47, An Italian Visit, Pegasus and Other Poems* and *The Gate and Other Poems*. His translation of *The Aeneid of Virgil* was first published in 1952 and is available in an Anchor Books edition.

The Eclogues and Georgics

of Virgil

TRANSLATED BY
C. DAY LEWIS

Anchor Books
Doubleday & Company, Inc.
Garden City, New York

CONTENTS

THE ECLOGUES

FOREWORD

I have used for the most part in this translation the same metre as I used in translating Virgil's *Georgics* and *Aeneid*—a metre with six stresses to the line. Though it is very different in its rhythms from Virgil's hexameter, this metre is still the nearest approximation to the original which I myself can manage, and it enables me to translate line for line with a minimum of padding or omission. I have ventured, however, to abandon this metre for the singing matches and songs in *Eclogues* 3, 5, 7 and 8: these I have rendered in the metrical pattern of certain English and Irish folk songs, and thus more freely than the rest of the text. Virgil wrote these passages too in hexameters; but the six-stress line in English cannot convey a singing effect, and I like songs to have tunes.

Virgil's *Eclogues* are the earliest Latin pastoral poetry. His master in this medium was the Sicilian Theocritus, who also wrote in hexameters. Today we are inclined to think of pastoral as a highly artificial kind of poetry, lacking in sincerity. The *Eclogues*—particularly the *Eighth,* which owes most to Theocritus—can be called artificial, but not in the sense that French and English imitations so often were. Virgil was not a court poet nor a city-dweller with romantic, 'escapist' ideas about the simple country life: he was a countryman himself, born on a farm near Mantua and living later a retired life in the south of Italy. His sympathy with nature is a countryman's sympathy, based on experience, not on wistful idealizing. He knew, as the *Georgics* show us, how hard is the existence of those who work on the land; and more than once in the *Eclogues* he writes about the predicament of country-dwellers forced to leave their homes, dispossessed by demobilized soldiers of the civil wars.

Although the *Eclogues* give us more of the charm than the harshness of rural life, beneath their pastoral conventions of disappointed love, nymphs and swains, flattery and flyting,

Arcadian rivalry in singing and in country pursuits, there is a solid ground of experience. We find here little of the realism of the *Georgics*, but there is sharp observation, humour and unforced emotion. In the famous *Fourth Eclogue*, where Virgil celebrates the consulship of his friend Pollio, a deeper note is struck which has allowed some to see this poem as prophetic of the birth of Christ; while in the *Sixth*—to me, the finest of them all—there is a magnificent passage about the Creation that reminds us how Virgil's greatest ambition, as he tells us in the *Georgics*, was to be a natural philosopher.

The world of the *Eclogues*, Dr. E. V. Rieu has said, is 'a world where everything is quick with understanding': nature, man and deity are interfused, responding to one another immediately and without self-consciousness. They are sincere, because Virgil had a deep feeling for this golden-age spirit and spontaneity, which for him still haunted the countryside. Professor Michael Grant summed up admirably the fascination of the *Eclogues* when he wrote, 'they display a satisfying and piquant balance, a harmonious contrast, between the simplicity of their subject and the artistry with which it is treated'.

C. D. L.

March 1962

This translation
is dedicated to
WILFRID COWLEY

ECLOGA I

Tityre, tu patulae recubans sub tegmine fagi
silvestrem tenui musam meditaris avena:
nos patriae finis et dulcia linquimus arva.
nos patriam fugimus: tu, Tityre, lentus in umbra
formosam resonare doces Amaryllida silvas.   5

O Meliboee, deus nobis haec otia fecit.
namque erit ille mihi semper deus, illius aram
saepe tener nostris ab ovilibus imbuet agnus.
ille meas errare boves, ut cernis, et ipsum
ludere quae vellem calamo permisit agresti.   10

Non equidem invideo: miror magis, undique totis
usque adeo turbamur agris. en, ipse capellas
protinus aeger ago: hanc etiam vix, Tityre, duco.
hic inter densas corylos modo namque gemellos,
spem gregis, a, silice in nuda conixa reliquit.   15
saepe malum hoc nobis, si mens non laeva fuisset,
de caelo tactas memini praedicere quercus.
sed tamen iste deus qui sit, da, Tityre, nobis.

Urbem, quam dicunt Romam, Meliboee, putavi
stultus ego huic nostrae similem, quo saepe solemus   20
pastores ovium teneros depellere fetus.
sic canibus catulos similis, sic matribus haedos
noram, sic parvis componere magna solebam.
verum haec tantum alias inter caput extulit urbes
quantum lenta solent inter viburna cupressi.   25

ECLOGUE 1

MELIBOEUS

Tityrus, here you loll, your slim reed-pipe serenading
The woodland spirit beneath a spread of sheltering beech,
While I must leave my home place, the fields so dear to me.
I'm driven from my home place: but you can take it easy
In shade and teach the woods to repeat 'Fair Amaryllis'.   5

TITYRUS

O Meliboeus, a god has given me this ease—
One who will always be a god to me, whose altar
I'll steep with the blood of many a tender lamb from my
    sheep-folds.
It's by his grace, you see, that my cattle browse and I
Can play whatever tunes I like on this country reed-pipe.   10

MELIBOEUS

Well, I don't grudge you that: but it does amaze me, when
Such a pack of troubles worry us countrymen everywhere.
On and on, sick-hearted, I drive my goats: look, this one
Can hardly move—in that hazel thicket she dropped her twin
    kids,
The hope of my flock, but she has to leave them upon bare
    flint.   15
Times enough, I know it, I was forewarned of this,
When lightning struck the oaks—my wits must have been
    addled.
But tell me about that god of yours, my friend: who is he?

TITYRUS

The city men call Rome—in my ignorance I used to
Imagine it like the market town to which we shepherds   20
Have so often herded the weanlings of our flocks.
Thus I came to know how dogs resemble puppies,
Goats their kids, and by that scale to compare large things
    with small.
But Rome carries her head as high above other cities
As cypresses tower over the tough wayfaring tree.   25

MELIBOEUS

Et quae tanta fuit Romam tibi causa videndi?

TITYRUS

Libertas, quae sera tamen respexit inertem,
candidior postquam tondenti barba cadebat,
respexit tamen et longo post tempore venit,
postquam nos Amaryllis habet, Galatea reliquit.   30
namque, fatebor enim, dum me Galatea tenebat,
nec spes libertatis erat nec cura peculi.
quamvis multa meis exiret victima saeptis,
pinguis et ingratae premeretur caseus urbi,
non umquam gravis aere domum mihi dextra redibat.   35

MELIBOEUS

Mirabar quid maesta deos, Amarylli, vocares,
cui pendere sua patereris in arbore poma:
Tityrus hinc aberat. ipsae te, Tityre, pinus,
ipsi te fontes, ipsa haec arbusta vocabant.

TITYRUS

Quid facerem? neque servitio me exire licebat   40
nec tam praesentis alibi cognoscere divos.
hic illum vidi iuvenem, Meliboee, quotannis
bis senos cui nostra dies altaria fumant.
hic mihi responsum primus dedit ille petenti:
'pascite ut ante boves, pueri; summittite tauros.'   45

MELIBOEUS

Fortunate senex, ergo tua rura manebunt.
et tibi magna satis, quamvis lapis omnia nudus
limosoque palus obducat pascua iunco:
non insueta gravis temptabunt pabula fetas,
nec mala vicini pecoris contagia laedent.   50
fortunate senex, hic inter flumina nota
et fontis sacros frigus captabis opacum.
hinc tibi, quae semper, vicino ab limite saepes

MELIBOEUS

What was the grand cause of your setting eyes on Rome, then?

TITYRUS

Freedom gave me a look—oh, long-delayed it was,
And I apathetic; my beard fell whiter now as I clipped it—
Still, she gave me that look and late in the day she came,
After my Galatea had left me, when Amaryllis   30
Possessed my heart. Believe me, while Galatea reigned
I had no chance of freedom, no attention to spare for savings:
Many a fatted beast I took to sell in the temple,
Many the rich cheeses I pressed for ungrateful townsfolk,
Yet never did I get home with much money in my pocket. 35

MELIBOEUS

I used to wonder why Amaryllis called so sadly
Upon the gods, and let her apple crop go hang.
Tityrus was not there. The very springs and pine-trees
Called out, these very orchards were crying for you, my friend.

TITYRUS

What was I to do? There was no way out from my
       slavery.   40
Nowhere else could I find a divine one ready to help me.
At Rome, Meliboeus, I saw that young prince in whose honour
My altar shall smoke twelve times a year. At Rome I made
My petition to him, and he granted it readily, saying, 'My lads,
Pasture your cattle, breed from your bulls, as you did of
       old'.   45

MELIBOEUS

Fortunate old man!—so your acres will be yours still.
They're broad enough for you. Never mind if it's stony soil
Or the marsh films over your pastureland with mud and
       rushes.
At least no queer vegetation will tempt your breeding ewes,
And there's no risk of their catching disease from a neigh-
       bour's flock.   50
Ah, fortunate old man, here among hallowed springs
And familiar streams you'll enjoy the longed-for shade, the
       cool shade.
Here, as of old, where your neighbour's land marches with
       yours,

Hyblaeis apibus florem depasta salicti
saepe levi somnum suadebit inire susurro: 55
hinc alta sub rupe canet frondator ad auras;
nec tamen interea raucae, tua cura, palumbes,
nec gemere aëria cessabit turtur ab ulmo.

TITYRUS

Ante leves ergo pascentur in aethere cervi,
et freta destituent nudos in litore piscis, 60
ante pererratis amborum finibus exsul
aut Ararim Parthus bibet aut Germania Tigrim,
quam nostro illius labatur pectore vultus.

MELIBOEUS

At nos hinc alii sitientis ibimus Afros,
pars Scythiam et rapidum cretae veniemus Oxum 65
et penitus toto divisos orbe Britannos.
en umquam patrios longo post tempore finis,
pauperis et tuguri congestum caespite culmen,
post aliquot, mea regna videns, mirabor aristas?
impius haec tam culta novalia miles habebit, 70
barbarus has segetes: en quo discordia civis
perduxit miseros! his nos consevimus agros!
insere nunc, Meliboee, piros; pone ordine vitis.
ite meae, quondam felix pecus, ite capellae.
non ego vos posthac viridi proiectus in antro 75
dumosa pendere procul de rupe videbo;
carmina nulla canam; non, me pascente, capellae,
florentem cytisum et salices carpetis amaras.

TITYRUS

Hic tamen hanc mecum poteras requiescere noctem
fronde super viridi: sunt nobis mitia poma, 80
castaneae molles et pressi copia lactis;
et iam summa procul villarum culmina fumant,
maioresque cadunt altis de montibus umbrae.

The sally hedge, with bees of Hybla sipping its blossom,
Shall often hum you gently to sleep. On the other side   55
Vine-dressers will sing to the breezes at the crag's foot;
And all the time your favourites, the husky-voiced wood
    pigeons
Shall coo away, and turtle doves make moan in the elm tops.

TITYRUS

Sooner shall lightfoot stags go grazing on thin air,
Or the sea contract, leaving its fishes high and dry;   60
Sooner the Germans and the Parthians, migrating
Across each other's frontiers, drink of each other's broad
Rivers, than I'll forget the look that young prince gave me.

MELIBOEUS

But the rest of us must go from here and be dispersed—
To Scythia, bone-dry Africa, the chalky spate of the
    Oxus,   65
Even to Britain—that place cut off at the very world's end.
Ah, when shall I see my native land again? after long years,
Or never?—see the turf-dressed roof of my simple cottage,
And wondering gaze at the ears of corn that were all my
    kingdom?
To think of some godless soldier owning my well-farmed
    fallow,   70
A foreigner reaping these crops! To such a pass has civil
√ Dissension brought us: for people like these we have sown
    our fields.
Well, graft your pears, Meliboeus, and set your vines in rows.
Move onward, little she-goats, onward, once-happy flock!
No more shall I, stretched out in some green dingle here,   75
Watch you poised far off on the bushy brows of a hillside.
No more singing for me, no taking you to browse,
My little goats, on bitter willow and clover flower.

TITYRUS

Yet surely you could rest with me tonight and sleep
On a bed of green leaves here? You're welcome to taste my
    mellow   80
Apples, my floury chestnuts, my ample stock of cheese.
Look over there—smoke rises already from the rooftops
And longer fall the shadows cast by the mountain heights.

ECLOGA II

Formosum pastor Corydon ardebat Alexim,
delicias domini; nec quid speraret habebat.
tantum inter densas, umbrosa cacumina, fagos
adsidue veniebat. ibi haec incondita solus
montibus et silvis studio iactabat inani: 5
  'O crudelis Alexi, nihil mea carmina curas?
nil nostri miserere? mori me denique coges.
nunc etiam pecudes umbras et frigora captant,
nunc viridis etiam occultant spineta lacertos,
Thestylis et rapido fessis messoribus aestu   10
alia serpyllumque herbas contundit olentis.
at mecum raucis, tua dum vestigia lustro,
sole sub ardenti resonant arbusta cicadis.
nonne fuit satius, tristis Amaryllidis iras
atque superba pati fastidia? nonne Menalcan,   15
quamvis ille niger, quamvis tu candidus esses?
o formose puer, nimium ne crede colori!
alba ligustra cadunt, vaccinia nigra leguntur.
  'despectus tibi sum, nec qui sim quaeris, Alexi,
quam dives pecoris, nivei quam lactis abundans.   20
mille meae Siculis errant in montibus agnae;
lac mihi non aestate novum, non frigore defit.
canto, quae solitus, si quando armenta vocabat,
Amphion Dircaeus in Actaeo Aracyntho.
nec sum adeo informis: nuper me in litore vidi,   25
cum placidum ventis staret mare; non ego Daphnim
iudice te metuam, si numquam fallit imago.

ECLOGUE 2

A shepherd, Corydon, burned with love for his master's
    favourite,
Handsome Alexis. Little reason had he for hope;
But he was always going into the beech plantation
Under whose spires and shades, alone with his futile passion,
He poured forth words like these, piecemeal, to wood and
    hill:—   5
'Cruel Alexis, can my sad airs mean nothing to you?
No pity for me? One day you'll drive me to my death.
Even the cattle now are making for cool shade,
Even the green lizards are hiding in thorn thickets,
And Thestylis prepares a pottage of savoury herbs,   10
Garlic and thyme, for harvesters whom the fierce heat has
    wearied.
But I trail in your footsteps under the blazing sun
While copses thrum with my hoarse voice and the cicada's.
I'd have done better to bear the sulks and rages, the insolent
Disdain of Amaryllis, or to make do with Menalcas,   15
Swarthy though he is, compared with your dazzling fairness.
Don't bank too much on your complexion, lovely boy—
Pale privet-blossom falls, no less than the dark-toned hyacinth.
  'Alexis, you look down on me; you never think
What I am—how rich in livestock, in wealth of snowy
    milk.   20
A thousand lambs of mine roam the Sicilian hills;
I never have run short of fresh milk, summer or winter.
I sing as, on a time, Amphion used to sing,
Calling his cattle home down the slopes of Aracynthus.
I'm not so ill-favoured, either: the other day on the shore,   25
When the sea's face was unfretted, I saw myself; if that mirror
Tells true, I could compete with Daphnis and win your
    verdict.

'o tantum libeat mecum tibi sordida rura
atque humilis habitare casas, et figere cervos,
haedorumque gregem viridi compellere hibisco!   30
mecum una in silvis imitabere Pana canendo.
Pan primus calamos cera coniungere pluris
instituit, Pan curat ovis oviumque magistros.
nec te paeniteat calamo trivisse labellum:
haec eadem ut sciret, quid non faciebat Amyntas?   35
est mihi disparibus septem compacta cicutis
fistula, Damoetas dono mihi quam dedit olim,
et dixit moriens: 'te nunc habet ista secundum':
dixit Damoetas, invidit stultus Amyntas.
praeterea duo nec tuta mihi valle reperti   40
capreoli, sparsis etiam nunc pellibus albo;
bina die siccant ovis ubera; quos tibi servo.
iam pridem a me illos abducere Thestylis orat;
et faciet, quoniam sordent tibi munera nostra.
'huc ades, o formose puer: tibi lilia plenis   45
ecce ferunt Nymphae calathis; tibi candida Nais,
pallentis violas et summa papavera carpens,
narcissum et florem iungit bene olentis anethi;
tum casia atque aliis intexens suavibus herbis
mollia luteola pingit vaccinia calta.   50
ipse ego cana legam tenera lanugine mala
castaneasque nuces, mea quas Amaryllis amabat;
addam cerea pruna (honos erit huic quoque pomo);
et vos, o lauri, carpam, et te, proxima myrte:
sic positae quoniam suavis miscetis odores.   55
'rusticus es, Corydon: nec munera curat Alexis,
nec, si muneribus certes, concedat Iollas.

'How wonderful it would be to live together in these
Rough fields, in a homely cottage, hunting the deer with our
  bows,
Herding a flock of kids with green marsh-mallow
  switches!   30
Here with me in the woodlands, you'd rival Pan for music.
Pan invented the shepherd's pipes, waxing a handful
Of reeds together: Pan looks after sheep and shepherd.
You'd never regret chafing your lip upon the pipes—
Think what Amyntas gladly suffered to learn the art.   35
I have an instrument—seven hemlock stalks of graded
Lengths went to its making: Damoetas gave it me
Long ago on his death bed, saying, "You'll be its second
And lucky slave." That boor, Amyntas, envied me.
What's more, I have two roes which I found in a dangerous
  combe—   40
Their hides have not yet lost the white markings: twice a day
  now
They're milking a ewe dry. I'm keeping them for you.
Thestylis has been begging for ages, to take them off me;
And she can have them, as you turn up your nose at my
  presents.
      'Handsome boy, come here! Look how the nymphs are
        bringing   45
Great basketfuls of lilies for you; for you the shining
Naiad picks a bunch of pale iris and poppy-heads,
Blends them with narcissus and the sweet-smelling anise,
Twines cassia in, and other fragrant herbs, and sets off
Unassuming blueberries with flamboyant marigold.   50
Myself will gather you quinces of pale and velvety bloom
And the chestnuts Amaryllis loved when she was mine;
Waxy-looking plums too—that fruit shall have its due;
And I'll cut branches of laurel, and of myrtle that grows near
  it—
Sweet is their mingled fragrance when they are put to-
  gether.   55
      'Bumpkin! as if Alexis cared twopence for your offerings!
And anyway, Iollas could beat you at present-giving.

heu heu, quid volui misero mihi? floribus Austrum
perditus et liquidis immisi fontibus apros.
quem fugis, a, demens? habitarunt di quoque silvas   60
Dardaniusque Paris. Pallas quas condidit arces
ipsa colat; nobis placeant ante omnia silvae.
torva leaena lupum sequitur, lupus ipse capellam,
florentem cytisum sequitur lasciva capella,
te Corydon, o Alexi: trahit sua quemque voluptas.   65
    'aspice, aratra iugo referunt suspensa iuvenci,
et sol crescentis decedens duplicat umbras:
me tamen urit amor: quis enim modus adsit amori?
    'a, Corydon, Corydon, quae te dementia cepit?
semiputata tibi frondosa vitis in ulmo est.   70
quin tu aliquid saltem potius, quorum indiget usus,
viminibus mollique paras detexere iunco?
invenies alium, si te hic fastidit, Alexim.'

Poor fool that I was, to have such daydreams. Now in my
    folly
I've let the wind get at my flowers, the boars muddy my
    spring.
Who are you running from, you crazy man? Why, Trojan   60
Paris, and even gods, have lived in the woods like me.
Let Athene dwell in the cities she's founded. For me, the
    woodlands.
Fierce lioness goes after wolf, wolf after goat,
The wanton goat goes after the flowering clover, and I
Go after you, Alexis—each towed by his own fancy.   65
   'Look, ploughs feather the ground as the ox-teams draw
    them home,
And a declining sun enlarges the lengthening shadows:
Yet love still scorches me—love has no lull, no limit.
   'Ah Corydon, Corydon, what is this lunacy you're pos-
    sessed by?
You've left your vines half-pruned, and the leafy elms they
    grow on.   70
Why not, instead of moping, get down to something useful,
Weaving from reeds and withies some article that you need?
If you're brushed off by this Alexis, you'll find another.'

ECLOGA III

MENALCAS
Dic mihi, Damoeta, cuium pecus? an Meliboei?
DAMOETAS
Non, verum Aegonis; nuper mihi tradidit Aegon.
MENALCAS
Infelix o semper oves, pecus! ipse Neaeram
dum fovet ac ne me sibi praeferat illa veretur,
hic alienus ovis custos bis mulget in hora,   5
et sucus pecori et lac subducitur agnis.
DAMOETAS
Parcius ista viris tamen obicienda memento.
novimus, et qui te, transversa tuentibus hircis,
et quo—sed faciles Nymphae risere—sacello.
MENALCAS
Tum, credo, cum me arbustum videre Miconis   10
atque mala vitis incidere falce novellas.
DAMOETAS
Aut hic ad veteres fagos cum Daphnidis arcum
fregisti et calamos: quae tu, perverse Menalca,
et cum vidisti puero donata, dolebas,
et si non aliqua nocuisses, mortuus esses.   15
MENALCAS
Quid domini faciant, audent cum talia fures?
non ego te vidi Damonis, pessime, caprum
excipere insidiis, multum latrante Lycisca?
et cum clamarem 'quo nunc se proripit ille?
Tityre, coge pecus!' tu post carecta latebas.   20

ECLOGUE 3

MENALCAS

Who owns that flock, Damoetas? Come, tell me. Meliboeus?

DAMOETAS

No, it belongs to Aegon: he's just left me in charge.

MENALCAS

Those sheep have nothing but bad luck! So Aegon, he goes off
To keep Neaera warm, for fear she prefers me
To him, while a hired hand milks them twice an hour—⠀⠀⠀5
Milks the ewes all dry, not a drop left for the lambs.

DAMOETAS

Watch it! What right have you to lecture a chap? We all know
What *you* did—even the he-goats looked shocked—and in a
⠀⠀⠀shrine too
(But the nymphs are easygoing, they only smiled at it.)

MENALCAS

Just as they smiled, I bet, when they saw me take a bill-
⠀⠀⠀hook⠀⠀⠀10
And slash at Micon's vineyard and maim his growing vines.

DAMOETAS

Or here, by this old plantation of beeches, when you smashed
Daphnis's bow and arrows. So malicious you are—seeing them
Given to the boy made you turn nasty; and you'd have died
Of spite, if you hadn't been able to take it out on him some-
⠀⠀⠀how.⠀⠀⠀15

MENALCAS

What can the master do, when thieves are grown so bold?
Oh yes, I saw you lurking to rustle a goat of Damon's,
You desperado, while his mongrel was barking its head off.
I shouted, 'What's he after now? Round up your flock,
Tityrus!' There you were, hiding among the rushes.⠀⠀⠀20

DAMOETAS

An mihi cantando victus non redderet ille
quem mea carminibus meruisset fistula caprum?
si nescis, meus ille caper fuit; et mihi Damon
ipse fatebatur; sed reddere posse negabat.

MENALCAS

Cantando tu illum? aut umquam tibi fistula cera   25
iuncta fuit? non tu in triviis, indocte, solebas
stridenti miserum stipula disperdere carmen?

DAMOETAS

Vis ergo inter nos quid possit uterque vicissim
experiamur? ego hanc vitulam (ne forte recuses,
bis venit ad mulctram, binos alit ubere fetus)   30
depono: tu dic mecum quo pignore certes.

MENALCAS

De grege non ausim quicquam deponere tecum:
est mihi namque domi pater, est iniusta noverca;
bisque die numerant ambo pecus, alter et haedos.
verum, id quod multo tute ipse fatebere maius—   35
insanire libet quoniam tibi—pocula ponam
fagina, caelatum divini opus Alcimedontis:
lenta quibus torno facili super addita vitis
diffusos hedera vestit pallente corymbos.
in medio duo signa, Conon, et—quis fuit alter,   40
descripsit radio totum qui gentibus orbem,
tempora quae messor, quae curvus arator haberet?
necdum illis labra admovi, sed condita servo.

DAMOETAS

Et nobis idem Alcimedon duo pocula fecit,
et molli circum est ansas amplexus acantho,   45
Orpheaque in medio posuit silvasque sequentis.
necdum illis labra admovi, sed condita servo.
si ad vitulam spectas, nihil est quod pocula laudes.

MENALCAS

Numquam hodie effugies; veniam quocumque vocaris.

DAMOETAS

Damon owed me a goat. I won it when I beat him
At piping and singing. So why didn't he hand it over?
In case you don't know, that goat was mine: Damon admitted
As much to me, but he said he couldn't afford to give it.

MENALCAS

You beat him at music? Have you ever owned a set   25
Of reed-pipes waxed together? You amateur, puffing a scrannel
Tune on a squeaky straw at the crossroads is more your mark!

DAMOETAS

All right! Let's have a match, each singing in turn, and try out
Each other's skill. For my part, I'll stake a heifer: she comes
Twice a day to be milked and suckles two calves besides—   30
So don't fight shy. And now let's hear what you can wager.

MENALCAS

Livestock I would not dare to gamble with at all.
You see, I have my father at home, and a harsh stepmother:
Twice a day both count the cattle, and one the kids too.
But, as you're mad enough to challenge me, I'll put up   35
Something even you will admit has greater value—
My beechwood cups which Alcimedon, the master-craftsman,
    carved.
Effortlessly he chiselled upon them a supple vine
And wreathed its branching clusters of grapes with livid ivy.
Two figures in between, Conon and—who's the other,   40
He that surveyed the heavens for humankind and told us
When to reap, and when to thrust forward over the plough?
Those cups I have never drunk from. I keep them stored
    away.

DAMOETAS

Well, come to that, Alcimedon made me a pair of cups too:
He coiled their handles round with soft acanthus leaves,   45
And in between carved Orpheus and the woods following him.
These cups I have never drunk from. I keep them stored away.
But, if you saw my heifer, you'd not boast of your cups.

MENALCAS

No getting away from me now! I'll meet you on your own
    ground.

audiat haec tantum—vel qui venit, ecce, Palaemon.   50
efficiam, posthac ne quemquam voce lacessas.

DAMOETAS

Quin age, si quid habes; in me mora non erit ulla,
nec quemquam fugio: tantum, vicine Palaemon,
sensibus haec imis—res est non parva—reponas.

PALAEMON

Dicite, quandoquidem in molli consedimus herba,   55
et nunc omnis ager, nunc omnis parturit arbos,
nunc frondent silvae, nunc formosissimus annus.
incipe, Damoeta; tu deinde sequere, Menalca.
alternis dicetis; amant alterna Camenae.

DAMOETAS

Ab Iove principium musae; Iovis omnia plena,   60
ille colit terras, illi mea carmina curae.

MENALCAS

Et me Phoebus amat; Phoebo sua semper apud me
munera sunt, lauri et suave rubens hyacinthus.

DAMOETAS

Malo me Galatea petit, lasciva puella,
et fugit ad salices et se cupit ante videri.   65

MENALCAS

At mihi sese offert ultro, meus ignis, Amyntas,
notior ut iam sit canibus non Delia nostris.

DAMOETAS

Parta meae Veneri sunt munera: namque notavi
ipse locum, aëriae quo congessere palumbes.

But we need a judge . . . and look, here comes Palaemon.
    Never   50
Again shall you irritate folk with your singing—I'll see to that.

DAMOETAS

Strike up, if you have a song to sing: I'll not be backward,
And no judge frightens me. But remember, neighbour Palae-
    mon,
This is a needle match, so listen with full attention.

PALAEMON

Then sing away. We sit upon the soft grass here   55
At the loveliest time of the year—fields pushing up their crops,
And every orchard fruiting and woodlands all in leaf.
You begin, Damoetas, and you, Menalcas, follow.
Sing turn and turn about: that's what the Muses love.

The Singing Match (tune: 'O Waly Waly')

DAMOETAS

From Jupiter my song begins
             for Jupiter is everywhere,   60
Making the earth all fruitful to be
             and to my ditties lending his ear.

MENALCAS

And I'm the man that Phoebus loves,
             my garden is Apollo's seat:
I give him gifts—the bay-tree and
             the hyacinth do blush so sweet.

DAMOETAS

Now Galatea throws at me
             an apple—she's a wanton maid:
Off to the sally trees she do run
             wishing I spy whereto she's fled.   65

MENALCAS

But dear Amyntas is my flame:
             he is my flame, and never coy.
My little dog, he knows the Moon,
             and just as well he knows that boy.

DAMOETAS

I have a present for my Venus,
             I've a present for my dear,
Since I did mark a tree top high
             and doves a-building nesties there.

MENALCAS

Quod potui, puero silvestri ex arbore lecta 70
aurea mala decem misi; cras altera mittam.

DAMOETAS

O quotiens et quae nobis Galatea locuta est!
partem aliquam, venti, divum referatis ad auris!

MENALCAS

Quid prodest quod me ipse animo non spernis, Amynta,
si, dum tu sectaris apros, ego retia servo? 75

DAMOETAS

Phyllida mitte mihi; meus est natalis, Iolla:
cum faciam vitulam pro frugibus, ipse venito.

MENALCAS

Phyllida amo ante alias: nam me discedere flevit,
et longum 'formose, vale, vale,' inquit, 'Iolla.'

DAMOETAS

Triste lupus stabulis, maturis frugibus imbres, 80
arboribus venti, nobis Amaryllidis irae.

MENALCAS

Dulce satis umor, depulsis arbutus haedis,
lenta salix feto pecori, mihi solus Amyntas.

DAMOETAS

Pollio amat nostram, quamvis est rustica, Musam:

MENALCAS

Ten golden apples did I pluck,
        ten golden apples a wild tree bore: 70
All that I could, I sent to my boy,
        tomorrow he shall have ten more.

DAMOETAS

Oh many times, oh charming words
        she's spoke to me, my Galatea!
Whisper a few, a few of them,
        you breezes, into heaven's ear!

MENALCAS

Ah what avails it, Amyntas dear,
        that after me your heart's inclined,
If while you hunt the ravening boar,
        you leave me the nets to mind?   75

DAMOETAS

Send Phyllis here, Iollas, do—
        send Phyllis here, for it's my birthday:
And when I sacrifice for the crops
        a heifer, come yourself this way.

MENALCAS

Phyllis I love before the rest,
        and Phyllis wept to see me go:
Long did she say farewell to me,
        farewell, farewell, my handsome beau.

DAMOETAS

The wolf is cruel to the sheep,
        cruel a storm to orchard tree,   80
Cruel is rain to ripened crops,
        Amaryllis' rage is cruel to me.

MENALCAS

A shower is sweet to growing crops,
        to weanling goats an arbutus tree;
Willow is sweet to breeding herds,
        none but Amyntas sweet to me.

DAMOETAS

My Muse is but a country girl,
        yet Pollio has sung her praise.

Pierides, vitulam lectori pascite vestro. 85

MENALCAS

Pollio et ipse facit nova carmina: pascite taurum,
iam cornu petat et pedibus qui spargat harenam.

DAMOETAS

Qui te, Pollio, amat, veniat quo te quoque gaudet;
mella fluant illi, ferat et rubus asper amomum.

MENALCAS

Qui Bavium non odit, amet tua carmina, Maevi, 90
atque idem iungat vulpes et mulgeat hircos.

DAMOETAS

Qui legitis flores et humi nascentia fraga,
frigidus, o pueri, fugite hinc, latet anguis in herba.

MENALCAS

Parcite, oves, nimium procedere: non bene ripae
creditur; ipse aries etiam nunc vellera siccat. 95

DAMOETAS

Tityre, pascentis a flumine reice capellas:
ipse, ubi tempus erit, omnis in fonte lavabo.

MENALCAS

Cogite ovis, pueri: si lac praeceperit aestus,
ut nuper, frustra pressabimus ubera palmis.

Fatten a calf, ye Muses all,
        for Pollio who loves your lays.   85

MENALCAS

But Pollio sings his own songs too:
        so feed a bullock for him, say I—
Fatten a bull with venturesome horns
        and hooves that make the soft sand fly.

DAMOETAS

May he who loves you, Pollio,
        delighting, share your paradise:
Let honey flow for him in streams
        and brambles bear a delicate spice.

MENALCAS

May he who loathes not Bavius be
        delighted, Maevius, by your ditties: 90
Let him yoke foxes to his plough,
        and milk he-goats that have no titties.

DAMOETAS

Oh children dear, who gather flowers,
        who gather flowers and wild strawberries
        near,
Run away quick—away from that grass,
        a cold cold snake is lurking there.

MENALCAS

Oh sheep, beware—graze not too far,
        and never trust that river bank:
Look at the ram, your leader, oh sheep,
        drying his fleece that still is dank.   95

DAMOETAS

Now Tityrus, keep back your goats
        from grazing near the river's brim:
I mean to dip them all in a pool—
        dip them myself, when comes the time.

MENALCAS

Now fold the flocks, my shepherd lads,
        for if the heat dries the milk again
As it has done these latter days,
        then we shall squeeze their teats all in vain.

DAMOETAS

Heu heu, quam pingui macer est mihi taurus in ervo! 100
idem amor exitium pecori pecorisque magistro.

MENALCAS

Hi certe—neque amor causa est—vix ossibus haerent.
nescio quis teneros oculus mihi fascinat agnos.

DAMOETAS

Dic, quibus in terris—et eris mihi magnus Apollo—
tris pateat caeli spatium non amplius ulnas. 105

MENALCAS

Dic, quibus in terris inscripti nomina regum
nascantur flores, et Phyllida solus habeto.

PALAEMON

Non nostrum inter vos tantas componere lites.
et vitula tu dignus et hic: et quisquis amores
aut metuet dulcis, aut experietur amaros. 110
claudite iam rivos, pueri: sat prata biberunt.

DAMOETAS

Ah my poor bull, he peaks and pines
　　　　though rich for him the vetches grow: 100
Love is the same for man or beast—
　　　　'tis death to herd and herdsman also.

MENALCAS

My flock are naught but skin and bone;
　　　　it is not love has injured my ewes:
Some evil eye has overlooked
　　　　my pretty lambs, I know not whose.

DAMOETAS

I have a riddle. Where on earth
　　　　is heaven only twelve feet broad?
Answer my riddle, and I'll say
　　　　Apollo's not a greater bard. 105

MENALCAS

I have a riddle. Where on earth
　　　　are flowers signed with kings' names grown?
Answer my riddle, and I'll say
　　　　that Phyllis shall be yours alone.

PALAEMON

I cannot decide between you, after so keen a contest.
Both of you deserve a heifer—and so does each man
Who trembles before love's sweetness or tastes her bitter
　　　rue. 110
Lads, let down the hatches, the fields have drunk their fill.

ECLOGA IV

Sicelides Musae, paulo maiora canamus!
non omnis arbusta iuvant humilesque myricae:
si canimus silvas, silvae sint consule dignae.
    Ultima Cumaei venit iam carminis aetas;
magnus ab integro saeclorum nascitur ordo.   5
iam redit et Virgo, redeunt Saturnia regna,
iam nova progenies caelo demittitur alto.
tu modo nascenti puero, quo ferrea primum
desinet ac toto surget gens aurea mundo,
casta fave Lucina: tuus iam regnat Apollo.   10
teque adeo decus hoc aevi, te consule, inibit,
Pollio, et incipient magni procedere menses;
te duce, si qua manent sceleris vestigia nostri,
inrita perpetua solvent formidine terras.
ille deum vitam accipiet divisque videbit   15
permixtos heroas, et ipse videbitur illis,
pacatumque reget patriis virtutibus orbem.
    At tibi prima, puer, nullo munuscula cultu
errantis hederas passim cum baccare tellus
mixtaque ridenti colocasia fundet acantho.   20
ipsae lacte domum referent distenta capellae
ubera, nec magnos metuent armenta leones:
ipsa tibi blandos fundent cunabula flores.
occidet et serpens, et fallax herba veneni
occidet; Assyrium vulgo nascetur amomum.   25

ECLOGUE 4

Sicilian Muse, I would try now a somewhat grander theme.
Shrubberies or meek tamarisks are not for all: but if it's
Forests I sing, may the forests be worthy of a consul.
　Ours is the crowning era foretold in prophecy:
Born of Time, a great new cycle of centuries　　　　　5
Begins. Justice returns to earth, the Golden Age
Returns, and its first-born comes down from heaven above.
Look kindly, chaste Lucina, upon this infant's birth,
For with him shall hearts of iron cease, and hearts of gold
Inherit the whole earth—yes, Apollo reigns now.　　　10
And it's while you are consul—you, Pollio—that this glorious
Age shall dawn, the march of its great months begin.
You at our head, mankind shall be freed from its age-long
　　　fear,
All stains of our past wickedness being cleansed away.
This child shall enter into the life of the gods, behold
　　　them　　　　　　　　　　　　　　　　　　15
Walking with antique heroes, and himself be seen of them,
And rule a world made peaceful by his father's virtuous acts.
　Child, your first birthday presents will come from nature's
　　　wild—
Small presents: earth will shower you with romping ivy,
　　　foxgloves,
Bouquets of gipsy lilies and sweetly-smiling acanthus.　　20
Goats shall walk home, their udders taut with milk, and
　　　nobody
Herding them: the ox will have no fear of the lion:
Silk-soft blossom will grow from your very cradle to lap you.
But snakes will die, and so will fair-seeming, poisonous plants.
Everywhere the commons will breathe of spice and in-
　　　cense.　　　　　　　　　　　　　　　　　　25

at simul heroum laudes et facta parentum
iam legere et quae sit poteris cognoscere virtus,
molli paulatim flavescet campus arista,
incultisque rubens pendebit sentibus uva,
et durae quercus sudabunt roscida mella.   30
pauca tamen suberunt priscae vestigia fraudis,
quae temptare Thetim ratibus, quae cingere muris
oppida, quae iubeant telluri infindere sulcos.
alter erit tum Tiphys, et altera quae vehat Argo
delectos heroas; erunt etiam altera bella,   35
atque iterum ad Troiam magnus mittetur Achilles.
    hinc, ubi iam firmata virum te fecerit aetas,
cedet et ipse mari vector, nec nautica pinus
mutabit merces: omnis feret omnia tellus.
non rastros patietur humus, non vinea falcem;   40
robustus quoque iam tauris iuga solvet arator;
nec varios discet mentiri lana colores,
ipse sed in pratis aries iam suave rubenti
murice, iam croceo mutabit vellera luto;
sponte sua sandyx pascentis vestiet agnos.   45
    'Talia saecla,' suis dixerunt, 'currite,' fusis
concordes stabili fatorum numine Parcae.
    adgredere o magnos—aderit iam tempus—honores,
cara deum suboles, magnum Iovis incrementum!
aspice convexo nutantem pondere mundum,   50
terrasque tractusque maris caelumque profundum!
aspice venturo laetantur ut omnia saeclo!
    o mihi tum longae maneat pars ultima vitae,
spiritus et quantum sat erit tua dicere facta,
non me carminibus vincat nec Thracius Orpheus,   55

But when you are old enough to read about famous men
And your father's deeds, to comprehend what manhood
    means,
Then a slow flush of tender gold shall mantle the great plains,
Then shall grapes hang wild and reddening on thorn-trees,
And honey sweat like dew from the hard bark of oaks.   30
Yet there'll be lingering traces still of our primal error,
Prompting us to dare the seas in ships, to girdle
Our cities round with walls and break the soil with plough-
    shares.
A second Argo will carry her crew of chosen heroes,
A second Tiphys steer her. And wars—yes, even wars   35
There'll be; and great Achilles must sail for Troy again.

    Later, when the years have confirmed you in full manhood,
Traders will retire from the sea, from the pine-built vessels
They used for commerce: every land will be self-supporting.
The soil will need no harrowing, the vine no pruning-knife; 40
And the tough ploughman may at last unyoke his oxen.
We shall stop treating wool with artificial dyes,
For the ram himself in his pasture will change his fleece's
    colour,
Now to a charming purple, now to a saffron hue,
And grazing lambs will dress themselves in coats of
    scarlet.   45
  'Run, looms, and weave this future!'—thus have the Fates
    spoken,
In unison with the unshakeable intent of Destiny.

    Come soon, dear child of the gods, Jupiter's great viceroy!
Come soon—the time is near—to begin your life illustrious!
Look how the round and ponderous globe bows to salute
    you,   50
The lands, the stretching leagues of sea, the unplumbed sky!
Look how the whole creation exults in the age to come!
    If but the closing days of a long life were prolonged
For me, and I with breath enough to tell your story,
Oh then I should not be worsted at singing by Thracian
    Orpheus   55

nec Linus, huic mater quamvis atque huic pater adsit,
Orphei Calliopea, Lino formosus Apollo.
Pan etiam, Arcadia mecum si iudice certet,
Pan etiam Arcadia dicat se iudice victum.

   incipe, parve puer, risu cognoscere matrem—   60
matri longa decem tulerunt fastidia menses.
incipe, parve puer: qui non risere parenti,
nec deus hunc mensa, dea nec dignata cubili est.

Or Linus—even though Linus were backed by Calliope
His mother, and Orpheus by his father, beauteous Apollo.
Should Pan compete with me, and Arcady judge us, even
Pan, great Pan, with Arcadian judges, would lose the contest.

    Begin, dear babe, and smile at your mother to show you
        know her—   60
This is the tenth month now, and she is sick of waiting.
Begin, dear babe. The boy who does not smile at his mother
Will never deserve to sup with a god or sleep with a goddess.

ECLOGA V

Cur non, Mopse, boni quoniam convenimus ambo,
tu calamos inflare levis, ego dicere versus,
hic corylis mixtas inter consedimus ulmos?

MOPSUS

Tu maior; tibi me est aequum parere, Menalca,
sive sub incertas Zephyris motantibus umbras,   5
sive antro potius succedimus. aspice, ut antrum
silvestris raris sparsit labrusca racemis.

MENALCAS

Montibus in nostris solus tibi certat Amyntas.

MOPSUS

Quid, si idem certet Phoebum superare canendo?

MENALCAS

Incipe, Mopse, prior, si quos aut Phyllidis ignis   10
aut Alconis habes laudes aut iurgia Codri.
incipe; pascentis servabit Tityrus haedos.

MOPSUS

Immo haec, in viridi nuper quae cortice fagi
carmina descripsi et modulans alterna notavi,
experiar: tu deinde iubeto ut certet Amyntas.   15

MENALCAS

Lenta salix quantum pallenti cedit olivae,
puniceis humilis quantum saliunca rosetis,
iudicio nostro tantum tibi cedit Amyntas.
sed tu desine plura, puer; successimus antro.

ECLOGUE 5

MENALCAS

Good-day to you, Mopsus. Now we have met here, both of us
    experts
—You at playing the light reed-pipe, and I at singing—
Let us sit down together in this grove of elm and hazel.

MOPSUS

You are the elder, Menalcas: it's for me to fall in with your
    wishes.
Shall we go under the trees, where light airs stir the
    shadows,   5
Or would you prefer a cave?—look, there is one, its opening
Festooned with hanging swags of wild vine, over there.

MENALCAS

No singer in these hills but Amyntas dares to challenge you.

MOPSUS

Yes, but Amyntas fancies himself to beat Apollo.

MENALCAS

Lead off with a song then, Mopsus—'The Loves of Phyllis',
    or   10
'In Alcon's Praise', or 'Quarrelsome Codrus'—any you know.
Lead off, and Tityrus here will look after our grazing kids.

MOPSUS

I'd rather try a song which I wrote the other day
On a green beech trunk, and set to music for voice and pipe
Antiphonally: let Amyntas improve on this, if he can.   15

MENALCAS

Well, in my view Amyntas compares with you no more
Than a dejected willow with the olive's silvery sheen,
Or the unassuming flower of valerian with red roses.
But here we are in the cave, my lad, so sing away.

MOPSUS

Exstinctum Nymphae crudeli funere Daphnim 20
flebant (vos coryli testes et flumina Nymphis),
cum complexa sui corpus miserabile nati,
atque deos atque astra vocat crudelia mater.
non ulli pastos illis egere diebus
frigida, Daphni, boves ad flumina; nulla neque amnem 25
libavit quadripes, nec graminis attigit herbam.
Daphni, tuum Poenos etiam gemuisse leones
interitum montesque feri silvaeque loquuntur.
Daphnis et Armenias curru subiungere tigris
instituit, Daphnis thiasos inducere Bacchi 30
et foliis lentas intexere mollibus hastas.
vitis ut arboribus decori est, ut vitibus uvae,
ut gregibus tauri, segetes ut pinguibus arvis,
tu decus omne tuis. postquam te fata tulerunt,
ipsa Pales agros atque ipse reliquit Apollo. 35
grandia saepe quibus mandavimus hordea sulcis,
infelix lolium et steriles nascuntur avenae;
pro molli viola, pro purpureo narcisso
carduus et spinis surgit paliurus acutis.
spargite humum foliis, inducite fontibus umbras, 40
pastores; mandat fieri sibi talia Daphnis;
et tumulum facite, et tumulo superaddite carmen:
'Daphnis ego in silvis, hinc usque ad sidera notus,
formosi pecoris custos, formosior ipse.'

MENALCAS

Tale tuum carmen nobis, divine poeta, 45
quale sopor fessis in gramine, quale per aestum
dulcis aquae saliente sitim restinguere rivo.
nec calamis solum aequiperas, sed voce magistrum.
fortunate puer, tu nunc eris alter ab illo.
nos tamen haec quocumque modo tibi nostra vicissim 50
dicemus, Daphnimque tuum tollemus ad astra;
Daphnim ad astra feremus: amavit nos quoque Daphnis.

Song (tune: 'The Lark in the Clear Air')

MOPSUS

Daphnis died. The nymphs bewailed his death—   20
        rivers and hazels heard them weeping:
'Cruel stars and gods!' his mother cried,
        clasping the poor corpse close in her arms.
No one drove his oxen to the stream,
        no beast ate or drank at all from sadness: 25
Even Afric lions roared their grief,
        forest and hill keened Daphnis dead.

Daphnis first enwreathed our wands with leaves,
        Daphnis was first to harness tigers,
Daphnis led the revellers through a dance—   30
        all for the Wine-god's festival day.
Vines grace elms, and grapes the vine,
        bulls grace herds and corn the joyous tillage:
Daphnis graced all nature—when he died,
        Corn-god and Song-god left us too.   35

Where we sowed our champion barley seed,
        darnel and wild oats choke the furrow:
Where sweet violets with narcissus grew,
        thistle and thorn are growing today.
Scatter leaves and shade the springs,   40
        raise a tomb (he asks) and write this upon
        it—
I lived in woods, my fame lives in the stars:
        lovely my flock was, lovelier I.

MENALCAS

What an inspired poet you are! To me, your singing   45
Is good as a sleep on the grass to a tired man, or a draught of
Fresh water from a dancing brook when the noonday parches
One's throat. My lucky lad, you are your master's equal
At piping and singing now; you'll be his worthy successor.
Still, I'll do what I can to make you some return   50
By way of this song, extolling your Daphnis to the stars—
Yes, I'll enstar Daphnis, for Daphnis loved me too.

MOPSUS

An quicquam nobis tali sit munere maius?
et puer ipse fuit cantari dignus, et ista
iam pridem Stimichon laudavit carmina nobis.   55

MENALCAS

Candidus insuetum miratur limen Olympi
sub pedibusque videt nubes et sidera Daphnis.
ergo alacris silvas et cetera rura voluptas
Panaque pastoresque tenet Dryadasque puellas.
nec lupus insidias pecori, nec retia cervis   60
ulla dolum meditantur: amat bonus otia Daphnis.
ipsi laetitia voces ad sidera iactant
intonsi montes; ipsae iam carmina rupes,
ipsa sonant arbusta: 'deus, deus ille, Menalca!'
sis bonus o felixque tuis! en quattuor aras: 65
ecce duas tibi, Daphni, duas altaria Phoebo.
pocula bina novo spumantia lacte quotannis
craterasque duo statuam tibi pinguis olivi,
et multo in primis hilarans convivia Baccho,
ante focum, si frigus erit, si messis, in umbra: 70
vina novum fundam calathis Ariusia nectar.
cantabunt mihi Damoetas et Lyctius Aegon;
saltantis Satyros imitabitur Alphesiboeus.
haec tibi semper erunt, et cum sollemnia vota
reddemus Nymphis, et cum lustrabimus agros.   75
dum iuga montis aper, fluvios dum piscis amabit,
dumque thymo pascentur apes, dum rore cicadae,
semper honos nomenque tuum laudesque manebunt.
ut Baccho Cererique, tibi sic vota quotannis
agricolae facient; damnabis tu quoque votis.   80

MOPSUS

Quae tibi, quae tali reddam pro carmine dona?
nam neque me tantum venientis sibilus Austri
nec percussa iuvant fluctu tam litora, nec quae

MOPSUS

Nothing you could give me would please me more than that;
For Daphnis, if any, deserved elegies; and besides,
Stimichon often has praised to me this song of yours.   55

Song (tune: the same)

MENALCAS

Daphnis shines at heaven's dazzling gate,
                    under his feet sees clouds and planets.
Shepherds, nymphs and Pan are glad for this,
                    forest and champaign quickened with joy.
Sheep nor deer have anything to dread—   60
                    wolf nor snare—for Daphnis loves the gentle:
Wooded hills, crags, orchards cry to heaven
                    jocund hymns—'A god is he!'

Bring us luck, good Daphnis! Here are two   65
                    altars for you, and two for Phoebus,
Where I'll set two bowls of olive oil,
                    two cups of creaming milk every year.
Ah, what feasts, what junketings there'll be
                    here in summer shade or winter fire-
                    light!   70
Wine shall flow, and friends shall sing for me,
                    Alphesiboeus dance like a faun.

These shall be your rites, whenever we
                    honour the nymphs or bless our acres.
Long as boars love heights and fish love streams,   75
                    long as cicadas sip at the dew,
Long as bees suck thyme—will you remain
                    praised and famed, our yearly vows re-
                    ceiving,
Binding us to make them good, the way
                    Corn-god and Wine-god also do.   80

MOPSUS

What, oh what can I do to reward you for such singing?
Sweeter it was to me than a south wind's rising murmur
Or the rhythmic drumming of waves on a beach; more sweet
    than the music

saxosas inter decurrunt flumina vallis.

MENALCAS

Hac te nos fragili donabimus ante cicuta. 85
haec nos 'formosum Corydon ardebat Alexim,'
haec eadem docuit 'cuium pecus? an Meliboei?'

MOPSUS

At tu sume pedum, quod, me cum saepe rogaret,
non tulit Antigenes (et erat tum dignus amari),
formosum paribus nodis atque aere, Menalca. 90

Rivulets make as they scamper down through rocky glens.

MENALCAS

But I will give you a present first—this delicate reed-pipe,   85
The one on which I learnt to play 'Handsome Alexis,
Corydon's Flame', and 'Tell me, is this Meliboeus' Flock?'

MOPSUS

And you shall have this beautiful crook, evenly studded
With bronze. Antigenes often asked me for it (and he was
Lovable then), but I would not part with it. Now it's
   yours.   90

ECLOGA VI

Prima Syracosio dignata est ludere versu
nostra neque erubuit silvas habitare Thalia.
cum canerem reges et proelia, Cynthius aurem
vellit et admonuit: 'pastorem, Tityre, pinguis
pascere oportet ovis, deductum dicere carmen.'   5
nunc ego—namque super tibi erunt qui dicere laudes,
Vare, tuas cupiant et tristia condere bella—
agrestem tenui meditabor harundine Musam.
non iniussa cano. si quis tamen haec quoque, si quis
captus amore leget, te nostrae, Vare, myricae,   10
te nemus omne canet; nec Phoebo gratior ulla est
quam sibi quae Vari praescripsit pagina nomen.
    Pergite, Pierides. Chromis et Mnasyllus in antro
Silenum pueri somno videre iacentem,
inflatum hesterno venas, ut semper, Iaccho: 15
serta procul tantum capiti delapsa iacebant,
et gravis attrita pendebat cantharus ansa.
adgressi—nam saepe senex spe carminis ambo
luserat—iniciunt ipsis ex vincula sertis.
addit se sociam timidisque supervenit Aegle,   20
Aegle, Naiadum pulcherrima, iamque videnti
sanguineis frontem moris et tempora pingit.
ille dolum ridens 'quo vincula nectitis?' inquit.

ECLOGUE 6

When I commenced poet, my Muse was not ashamed
To live in the woods and dally with lightweight pastoral verse.
Next, kings and wars possessed me; but Apollo tweaked my
    ear,
Telling me, 'Tityrus, a countryman should be
Concerned to put flesh on his sheep and keep his poetry
    spare.'   5
Since there'll be bards in plenty desiring to rehearse
Varus' fame, and celebrate the sorrowful theme of warfare,
I shall take up a slim reed-pipe and a rural subject;
And not unasked. If anyone—if a single reader falls
In love with this little poem of mine, it is you, Varus,   10
Our tamarisks, all our woods, will be singing about. No page
Could charm Apollo more than a page inscribed to Varus.
    Muses, begin! . . . Two boys, called Chromis and
    Mnasyllus,
Came upon old Silenus lying asleep in a cave,
His veins—as usual—swollen thick with yesterday's drink-
    ing: 15
The garlands had slid from his head to the floor, and a
    weighty wine-jar
Dangled from the fingers that had worn its handle thin.
Creeping close—for Silenus had often teased them both
With the hope of a song—they tied him up in his own gar-
    lands.
Then, as they shrank at their daring, Aegle, fairest of all   20
The Naiads, joined in and led them on, rougeing his brow
And temples with mulberry juice. But his eyes by now were
    open.
He smiled at their trick. 'Fetters?' he said, 'why fetter me?

'solvite me, pueri; satis est potuisse videri.
carmina quae vultis cognoscite; carmina vobis,   25
huic aliud mercedis erit.' simul incipit ipse.
tum vero in numerum Faunosque ferasque videres
ludere, tum rigidas motare cacumina quercus:
nec tantum Phoebo gaudet Parnasia rupes,
nec tantum Rhodope miratur et Ismarus Orphea.   30
   Namque canebat uti magnum per inane coacta
semina terrarumque animaeque marisque fuissent
et liquidi simul ignis; ut his exordia primis
omnia et ipse tener mundi concreverit orbis;
tum durare solum et discludere Nerea ponto   35
coeperit et rerum paulatim sumere formas;
iamque novum terrae stupeant lucescere solem,
altius atque cadant summotis nubibus imbres;
incipiant silvae cum primum surgere, cumque
rara per ignaros errent animalia montis.   40
   hinc lapides Pyrrhae iactos, Saturnia regna,
Caucasiasque refert volucris furtumque Promethei.
his adiungit, Hylan nautae quo fonte relictum
clamassent, ut litus 'Hyla, Hyla' omne sonaret;
et fortunatam, si numquam armenta fuissent,   45
Pasiphaen nivei solatur amore iuvenci.
a, virgo infelix, quae te dementia cepit?
Proetides implerunt falsis mugitibus agros,
at non tam turpis pecudum tamen ulla secuta est
concubitus, quamvis collo timuisset aratrum,   50
et saepe in levi quaesisset cornua fronte.
a, virgo infelix, tu nunc in montibus erras:
ille latus niveum molli fultus hyacintho
ilice sub nigra pallentis ruminat herbas,
aut aliquam in magno sequitur grege. 'claudite, Nymphae,

You've shown you can capture me. Enough. Now let me
    loose, lads.
I'll sing to you, as you want: the song is for you—a dif-
    ferent   25
Treat is in store for Aegle.' Straight off, he began singing.
You could have seen the fauns and every wild thing caper
In time to his music then, and the stiff oaks bow their heads—
Truly you could. Apollo gives not such joy to Parnassus:
Ismarus nor Rhodope are so enchanted by Orpheus.   30
    He sang Creation's birth—how seeds of earth and air,
Of water and fluent fire were brought together and married
In a vastness of empty space; how everything began
From this, and what were gases condensed to form our globe.
How next the land grew gradually more solid, and began   35
To put the seas in their place and shape the world we know;
And then the earth was dazed by unfamiliar sunshine,
The ceiling of cloud lifted and showers had further to fall,
Forests began their growth, animals here and there
To wander among the hills that never before had known
    them.   40
    He sang of Pyrrha, magicking stones into men; of Saturn's
Reign; of Prometheus tortured by eagles for stealing fire;
And Hylas—how the Argonauts left him beside a spring,
Then shouted for him till the whole shore was echoing 'Hylas!
    Hylas!'
Pasiphaë next he sang, appeasing her lust for a white bull— 45
Better for her, indeed, if cattle had never existed.
Ah, misfortunate girl, what madness was it possessed you?
Even the daughters of Proteus who, fancying they were
    heifers,
Mooed through the fields and shrank from the touch of a yoke
    and kept on
Feeling their smooth foreheads, expecting to find horns— 50
Not one of them, for all that, desired so bestial a mating.
Ah, misfortunate girl, you ramble among the hills now,
While he, your love, weighs down with snow-white flanks
    upon yielding
Hyacinth, chews the cud beneath some glooming ilex,
Or else he is chasing one of his heifers. 'Cretan nymphs!' 55

Dictaeae Nymphae, nemorum iam claudite saltus,   56
si qua forte ferant oculis sese obvia nostris
errabunda bovis vestigia; forsitan illum
aut herba captum viridi aut armenta secutum
perducant aliquae stabula ad Gortynia vaccae.'   60
    tum canit Hesperidum miratam mala puellam;
tum Phaethontiadas musco circumdat amarae
corticis, atque solo proceras erigit alnos.
tum canit errantem Permessi ad flumina Gallum
Aonas in montis ut duxerit una sororum,   65
utque viro Phoebi chorus adsurrexerit omnis;
ut Linus haec illi divino carmine pastor
floribus atque apio crinis ornatus amaro
dixerit: 'hos tibi dant calamos, en accipe, Musae,
Ascraeo quos ante seni, quibus ille solebat   70
cantando rigidas deducere montibus ornos.
his tibi Grynei nemoris dicatur origo,
ne quis sit lucus quo se plus iactet Apollo.'
    quid loquar aut Scyllam Nisi, quam fama secuta est
candida succinctam latrantibus inguina monstris   75
Dulichias vexasse rates et gurgite in alto,
a, timidos nautas canibus lacerasse marinis:
aut ut mutatos Terei narraverit artus,
quas illi Philomela dapes, quae dona pararit,
quo cursu deserta petiverit et quibus alte   80
infelix sua tecta super volitaverit alis?
    omnia, quae Phoebo quondam meditante beatus
audiit Eurotas iussitque ediscere lauros,
ille canit—pulsae referunt ad sidera valles.
cogere donec ovis stabulis numerumque referre   85
iussit et invito processit Vesper Olympo.

Pasiphaë cries, 'oh hurry! Close up the woodland rides!
There's still a hope that somewhere my eyes may chance upon
The tracks of his stravagueing hoof: perhaps my bull was
Lured by a lush green pasture, or he is with the herd
And some of the heifers will get him at last back to the
    steadings.'   60
   Next he sang of the girl who was greedy for an apple
From the Hesperides; and of Phaethon's sisters, enchanted
Into tall alders, prisoned in bitter, mossy bark.
And then he sang how Gallus, at large by the streams of
    Permessus,
Met one of the Muses, who led him to the Aonian hills   65
Where the whole choir of Apollo stood up to honour him,
A mortal; and that divine poet of pastoral, Linus,
Wearing his wreath of flowers and bitter parsley leaves,
Said to Gallus, 'the Muses give you this pipe—accept it—
Which long ago they gave to Hesiod; and he played it   70
So well, his music drew downhill the obstinate ash-trees.
Sing, to this pipe, the story of the Grynean wood,
And not one grove on earth will Apollo be so proud of.'
   Still he sang on: how Scylla, daughter of Nisus (pictured
In fable, she's fair but she wears a loincloth of baying mon-
    sters),   75
Hunted Odysseus' ships and with those sea-hounds' fangs
Horribly savaged his wincing men deep down in the whirl-
    pool.
. . . And still sang on—the legend of Tereus' transformation,
The food Philomela cooked him, the gifts she prepared him
    next,
The wings on which that luckless lady hovered above   80
Her palace roof and then made off into the desert.
   All the songs that of old time his favoured river, Eurotas,
Heard Apollo compose and made its laurels learn,
Silenus sang. The valleys caught this music and tossed it
Skyward. At last the Evening Star, unwelcome, rose   85
In heaven, bidding the boys drive home their sheep and
    count them.

ECLOGA VII

MELIBOEUS

Forte sub arguta consederat ilice Daphnis,
compulerantque greges Corydon et Thyrsis in unum,
Thyrsis ovis, Corydon distentas lacte capellas,
ambo florentes aetatibus, Arcades ambo,
et cantare pares et respondere parati.   5
huc mihi, dum teneras defendo a frigore myrtos,
vir gregis ipse caper deerraverat, atque ego Daphnim
aspicio. ille ubi me contra videt, 'ocius,' inquit,
'huc ades, o Meliboee; caper tibi salvus et haedi;
et, si quid cessare potes, requiesce sub umbra.   10
huc ipsi potum venient per prata iuvenci;
hic viridis tenera praetexit harundine ripas
Mincius, eque sacra resonant examina quercu.'
quid facerem? neque ego Alcippen nec Phyllida habebam
depulsos a lacte domi quae clauderet agnos,   15
et certamen erat, Corydon cum Thyrside, magnum.
posthabui tamen illorum mea seria ludo.
alternis igitur contendere versibus ambo
coepere; alternos Musae meminisse volebant.
hos Corydon, illos referebat in ordine Thyrsis.   20

CORYDON

Nymphae, noster amor, Libethrides, aut mihi carmen
quale meo Codro concedite (proxima Phoebi

ECLOGUE 7

It happened one day, when Daphnis had sat down under a
    rustling
Ilex, that Corydon and Thyrsis drove their flocks
Together—Corydon, his goats heavy with milk,
Thyrsis, his sheep. They were both in the flower of their
    youth, Arcadians,
Both ready to sing at the drop of a hat, or take a tune up.   5
Just then, I was lagging my delicate myrtles against the cold:
The he-goat, lord of my flock, wandered their way, so I
    noticed
Daphnis, who saw me too and called out, 'Quick, Meliboeus,
Come over here, if you've time to take a breather, and rest
In the shade with us. Your goat and kids will be safe
    enough;   10
Your bullocks will find their own way across the fields, do
    they need
To drink. The grassy banks of the Mincius are fringed here
With swaying reeds, and the sacred oak is a-drone with bees.'
What should I do? I had no Phyllis or Alcippe
At home to pen my lambs, which were newly weaned; but
    a singing   15
Match between Corydon and Thyrsis would be a great thing.
Well, in the end my work came second to their pastime.
So then the pair of them began to sing—in alternate
Stanzas, for that was how their Muse loved to arrange it—
Corydon first, and Thyrsis singing his antiphon.   20

Song (tune: 'The Banks of Sweet Primroses')

You nymphs I love, let me sing like Codrus,
         for he's my friend and a singer divine:

versibus ille facit) aut, si non possumus omnes,
hic arguta sacra pendebit fistula pinu.

THYRSIS

Pastores, hedera crescentem ornate poetam,   25
Arcades, invidia rumpantur ut ilia Codro;
aut, si ultra placitum laudarit, baccare frontem
cingite, ne vati noceat mala lingua futuro.

CORYDON

Saetosi caput hoc apri tibi, Delia, parvus
et ramosa Micon vivacis cornua cervi.   30
si proprium hoc fuerit, levi de marmore tota
puniceo stabis suras evincta coturno.

THYRSIS

Sinum lactis et haec te liba, Priape, quotannis
exspectare sat est: custos es pauperis horti.
nunc te marmoreum pro tempore fecimus; at tu,   35
si fetura gregem suppleverit, aureus esto.

CORYDON

Nerine Galatea, thymo mihi dulcior Hyblae,
candidior cycnis, hedera formosior alba,
cum primum pasti repetent praesepia tauri,
si qua tui Corydonis habet te cura, venito.   40

THYRSIS

Immo ego Sardoniis videar tibi amarior herbis,
horridior rusco, proiecta vilior alga,
si mihi non haec lux toto iam longior anno est.
ite domum pasti, si quis pudor, ite iuvenci.

CORYDON

Muscosi fontes et somno mollior herba,   45
et quae vos rara viridis tegit arbutus umbra,
solstitium pecori defendite: iam venit aestas
torrida, iam lento turgent in palmite gemmae.

THYRSIS

Hic focus et taedae pingues, hic plurimus ignis
semper et adsidua postes fuligine nigri: 50

But, if his music can have no rival,
>> I'll leave my shrill flute to hang on your pine.

THYRSIS

You shepherds, crown me your budding singer—   25
>> let Codrus burst with jealousy:

Or if he flatter me, wreathe him with foxgloves
>> lest sugary words harm your bard to be.

CORYDON

Diana, take this bristling boar's head,
>> these full-grown antlers from my hand: 30

If my luck lasts, a statue all marble,
>> red-booted for hunting, here you shall stand.

THYRSIS

Priapus, honey cakes and a bowl of
>> milk are all I can give you each year:

My garden is poor which you grace in mere marble—   35
>> if my flock prospers, in gold you'll be there.

CORYDON

More sweet than thyme, more fair than pale ivy,
>> more white than swans you are to me:

Come soon, when the bulls through the meadows are hom-
>> ing,

>> come soon, if you love me, my nymph of the
>> sea!
>> 40

THYRSIS

More tart than foreign herbs you may call me,
>> more rough than broom, more cheap than
>> sea-wrack,

If today has not dragged like a year for me. Home then—
>> for shame, you are gorged now, my heifers—
>> go back!

CORYDON

Oh mossy springs, grass soft as sleep is,   45
>> all besprent with green arbutus shade,

Cherish our sheep when the dog-days are on them:
>> summer is near now, the vine buds dilate.

THYRSIS

Oh here's a hearth and pine logs in plenty,
>> doorposts black with winter-long smoke: 50

hic tantum Boreae curamus frigora quantum
aut numerum lupus aut torrentia flumina ripas.

CORYDON

Stant et iuniperi et castaneae hirsutae,
strata iacent passim sua quaque sub arbore poma:
omnia nunc rident; at si formosus Alexis   55
montibus his abeat, videas et flumina sicca.

THYRSIS

Aret ager; vitio moriens sitit aëris herba;
Liber pampineas invidit collibus umbras:
Phyllidis adventu nostrae nemus omne virebit,
Iuppiter et laeto descendet plurimus imbri.   60

CORYDON

Populus Alcidae gratissima, vitis Iaccho,
formosae myrtus Veneri, sua laurea Phoebo;
Phyllis amat corylos; illas dum Phyllis amabit,
nec myrtus vincet corylos nec laurea Phoebi.

THYRSIS

Fraxinus in silvis pulcherrima, pinus in hortis,   65
populus in fluviis, abies in montibus altis:
saepius at si me, Lycida formose, revisas,
fraxinus in silvis cedat tibi, pinus in hortis.

MELIBOEUS

Haec memini, et victum frustra contendere Thyrsim.
ex illo Corydon Corydon est tempore nobis.   70

What are sheep-hordes to wolf, or high banks to flood-water?
　　　　what do we care for the north wind's cold
　　　　　　stroke?

CORYDON

Here chestnuts grow and juniper bushes,
　　　　round every tree's foot its windfalls lie:
All nature smiles, but if handsome Alexis　　　　55
　　　　goes from these hills, even the streams may
　　　　　　run dry.

THYRSIS

The fields are dry, a blight's in the weather,
　　　　no vine leaves grow—the Wine-god is sour—
Shading our uplands; but when my Phyllis comes here,
　　　　green shall the woodlands be, and many the
　　　　　　shower.　　　　60

CORYDON

For Bacchus, vines; for Hercules, poplar;
　　　　for Venus, myrtle; for Apollo, his bays:
Phyllis loves hazels—so long as she loves them,
　　　　bay-tree nor myrtle shall get more praise.

THYRSIS

Ash queens in woods, and stone-pine in gardens,　　　　65
　　　　by streams the poplar, on heights the fir-tree:
If Lycidas only were with me more often,
　　　　ash-tree and pine would be nothing to me.

MELIBOEUS

So I recall it. Thyrsis—he sang his best, and was beaten.
Since then, it has been all Corydon, all Corydon, for us.　　　　70

ECLOGA VIII

Pastorum Musam Damonis et Alphesiboei,
immemor herbarum quos est mirata iuvenca
certantis, quorum stupefactae carmine lynces,
et mutata suos requierunt flumina cursus,
Damonis Musam dicemus et Alphesiboei.   5

   Tu mihi seu magni superas iam saxa Timavi,
sive oram Illyrici legis aequoris,—en erit umquam
ille dies, mihi cum liceat tua dicere facta?
en erit ut liceat totum mihi ferre per orbem
sola Sophocleo tua carmina digna coturno?   10
a te principium, tibi desinet. accipe iussis
carmina coepta tuis, atque hanc sine tempora circum
inter victricis hederam tibi serpere lauros.

   Frigida vix caelo noctis decesserat umbra,
cum ros in tenera pecori gratissimus herba: 15
incumbens tereti Damon sic coepit olivae.

DAMON

   Nascere, praeque diem veniens age, Lucifer, almum,
coniugis indigno Nysae deceptus amore
dum queror, et divos, quamquam nil testibus illis
profeci, extrema moriens tamen adloquor hora.   20
   incipe Maenalios mecum, mea tibia, versus.
Maenalus argutumque nemus pinusque loquentis
semper habet; semper pastorum ille audit amores
Panaque, qui primus calamos non passus inertis.
   incipe Maenalios mecum, mea tibia, versus.   25

ECLOGUE 8

Let us honour the pastoral Muse of Damon and Alphesiboeus,
Whose singing, when they competed together, left the lynxes
Dumbfounded, caused a heifer to pause in her grazing, spell-
    bound,
And so entranced the rivers that they checked their onward
    flow.
Let us celebrate the Muse of Damon and Alphesiboeus.   5
  But, Pollio, where are you now?—shooting Timavus' rapids?
Coasting the shores of Illyria? Will ever the day come
When I shall be allowed to write about your exploits?
Ah, when will come the day when I may publish abroad
The worth of your plays, that alone can challenge Soph-
    ocles'?   10
You, my poetry's source, shall be its bourne. Accept
This poem—you bade me write it—and let the poet's ivy
Be threaded with the victor's laurels to crown your head . . .
  Night's chilly dark had only just faded in the sky—
At the dewfall hour when to cattle the tender grass tastes
    sweetest.   15
Leaning against an olive's smooth trunk, Damon began:—

Song (tune: 'Boolavogue')

DAMON
O morning star, bring the daylight charming
                while I, love's dupe, sing a dying plea:
Our vows were cheating, the gods unheeding—   20
                O flute of Maenalus, come, play for me!
On Maenalus are pine-woods sighing
                and shepherds crying their love all day:
'Tis Pan's abode, who made reeds melodious
                O flute of Maenalus, come, play for me!   25

Mopso Nysa datur: quid non speremus amantes?
iungentur iam grypes equis, aevoque sequenti
cum canibus timidi venient ad pocula dammae.
Mopse, novas incide faces: tibi ducitur uxor:
sparge, marite, nuces; tibi deserit Hesperus Oetam.   30
   incipe Maenalios mecum, mea tibia, versus.
o digno coniuncta viro, dum despicis omnis,
dumque tibi est odio mea fistula, dumque capellae
hirsutumque supercilium promissaque barba,
nec curare deum credis mortalia quemquam—   35
   incipe Maenalios mecum, mea tibia, versus.
saepibus in nostris parvam te roscida mala
(dux ego vester eram) vidi cum matre legentem.
alter ab undecimo tum me iam acceperat annus;
iam fragilis poteram a terra contingere ramos: 40
ut vidi, ut perii, ut me malus abstulit error!
   incipe Maenalios mecum, mea tibia, versus.
nunc scio quid sit Amor: duris in cotibus illum
aut Tmaros aut Rhodope aut extremi Garamantes
nec generis nostri puerum nec sanguinis edunt.   45
   incipe Maenalios mecum, mea tibia, versus.
saevus Amor docuit natorum sanguine matrem
commaculare manus; crudelis tu quoque, mater.
crudelis mater magis, an puer improbus ille?
   incipe Maenalios mecum, mea tibia, versus.   50
nunc et ovis ultro fugiat lupus, aurea durae

My girl's another's. The hopes of lovers
                    are wild and witless. Aye, griffins may
Yet mate with mares, and the timorous she-deer
                    may share a drinking trough with hounds,
             one day.
So lop your wedding torches, Mopsus,
                    and strew the nuts—your bride is she:
For you and Nysa the Eve-star rises—   30
                    O flute of Maenalus, come, play for me!

A proper splicing! for she despises
                    all men, does Nysa; but most of all
It's me she loathes—my flute, my goat flock,
                    my uncouth face with its long beard asprawl:
My brows untended, how they offend her!
                    No use to tell her God oversees
The world of mortals and woman's falseness—   35
                    O flute of Maenalus, come, play for me!

A child you were when I first beheld you—
                    our orchard fruit was chilled with dew—
You and your mother both apple-gathering:
                    just twelve I was, but I took charge of you.
On tiptoe reaching the laden branches,
                    one glance I gave you, and utterly   40
My heart was ravished, my reason banished—
                    O flute of Maenalus, come, play for me!

I know what Love is—too well I know him:
                    no boy of flesh and blood is he,
But hard as rock and harsh as deserts—   45
                    O flute of Maenalus, come, play for me!
When Cupid tempted, one slew her children—
                    could any mother so cruel be?
But which is crueller, she or Cupid?
                    O flute of Maenalus, come, play for me! 50

All is awry now. The wolf may fly from
                    the lamb, and oak trees bear fruit of gold;

mala ferant quercus, narcisso floreat alnus,
pinguia corticibus sudent electra myricae,
certent et cycnis ululae, sit Tityrus Orpheus,
Orpheus in silvis, inter delphinas Arion—   55
    incipe Maenalios mecum, mea tibia, versus.
omnia vel medium fiat mare. vivite, silvae:
praeceps aërii specula de montis in undas
deferar; extremum hoc munus morientis habeto.
    desine Maenalios, iam desine, tibia, versus.   60
    Haec Damon: vos, quae responderit Alphesiboeus,
dicite, Pierides; non omnia possumus omnes.

ALPHESIBOEUS

    Effer aquam, et molli cinge haec altaria vitta,
verbenasque adole pinguis et mascula tura,
coniugis ut magicis sanos avertere sacris   65
experiar sensus; nihil hic nisi carmina desunt.
    ducite ab urbe domum, mea carmina, ducite Daphnim.
carmina vel caelo possunt deducere Lunam;
carminibus Circe socios mutavit Vlixi;
frigidus in pratis cantando rumpitur anguis.   70
    ducite ab urbe domum, mea carmina, ducite Daphnim.
terna tibi haec primum triplici diversa colore
licia circumdo, terque haec altaria circum
effigiem duco; numero deus impare gaudet.
    ducite ab urbe domum, mea carmina, ducite Daphnim.   75
necte tribus nodis ternos, Amarylli, colores;

Alders surprise us with sweet narcissus,
        and tears of amber down a tamarisk roll.
Let screech-owl's flyting be more delightful
        than swan-song, Tityrus in minstrelsy
With Orpheus vying or with Orion—   55
        O flute of Maenalus, come, play for me!

Let Ocean swallow the land. Farewell, O
        my woods. I'll hurl me into the sea
From yonder peak. This last song for Nysa—
        O flute of Maenalus, now cease with me! 60

So Damon sang. What response was made by Alphesiboeus,
The Muses of Song must tell us—we cannot all do all things.

Song (tune: 'The Old Head of Dennis')
        ALPHESIBOEUS
Bring me water, and wool-wreaths to garland the shrine.
Bring vervain and masculine incense as well.
My love he is cold, some witchcraft I'll try   65
To make him catch fire: all I need is a spell.
Make Daphnis come home from the city, my spells!

Magic spells can inveigle the moon from the sky;
With her magic did Circe transform into beasts
The men of Ulysses; and magic can blast
A cold-clammy snake as it slides through the meads.   70
Make Daphnis come home now, come home now, my spells!

I have fashioned an image of Daphnis. Three threads
Of three different colours about it I lace.
Then bearing this mommet I've fashioned, three times—
Odd numbers bring luck—round the altar I pace.
Make Daphnis come home from the city, my spells!   75

Amaryllis, now plait you and fasten the threads—
These tricoloured threads in a triplicate knot:
And while, Amaryllis, you're twining them, chant

necte, Amarylli, modo, et 'Veneris,' dic, 'vincula necto.'
    ducite ab urbe domum, mea carmina, ducite Daphnim.
limus ut hic durescit, et haec ut cera liquescit
uno eodemque igni, sic nostro Daphnis amore.   80
sparge molam, et fragilis incende bitumine lauros.
Daphnis me malus urit, ego hanc in Daphnide laurum.
    ducite ab urbe domum, mea carmina, ducite Daphnim.
talis amor Daphnim, qualis cum fessa iuvencum
per nemora atque altos quaerendo bucula lucos   85
propter aquae rivum viridi procumbit in ulva
perdita, nec serae meminit decedere nocti,
talis amor teneat, nec sit mihi cura mederi.
    ducite ab urbe domum, mea carmina, ducite Daphnim.
has olim exuvias mihi perfidus ille reliquit,   90
pignora cara sui: quae nunc ego limine in ipso,
terra, tibi mando; debent haec pignora Daphnim.
    ducite ab urbe domum, mea carmina, ducite Daphnim.
has herbas atque haec Ponto mihi lecta venena
ipse dedit Moeris (nascuntur plurima Ponto);   95
his ego saepe lupum fieri et se condere silvis
Moerim, saepe animas imis excire sepulcris,
atque satas alio vidi traducere messis.
    ducite ab urbe domum, mea carmina, ducite Daphnim.
fer cineres, Amarylli, foras rivoque fluenti   100
transque caput iace, nec respexeris. his ego Daphnim
adgrediar; nihil ille deos, nil carmina curat.
    ducite ab urbe domum, mea carmina, ducite Daphnim.
aspice: corripuit tremulis altaria flammis
sponte sua, dum ferre moror, cinis ipse. bonum sit!   105
nescio quid certe est, et Hylax in limine latrat.
credimus? an, qui amant, ipsi sibi somnia fingunt?
    parcite, ab urbe venit, iam parcite carmina, Daphnis.

This cantrip—'It's Venus's chains that I plait.'
Make Daphnis come home now, come home now, my spells!

Like this clay growing hard and this wax melting soft
In the same fire, may Daphnis feel my love's fierce blaze.   80
Scatter salt grain, kindle bay-leaves to crackle with pitch.
For Daphnis I burn, let him burn like these bays.
Make Daphnis come home from the city, my spells!

As a heifer, long searching the woods for her mate,   85
Tired, hopeless, sinks down on the sedge by a stream,
And moves not, though night fall, so Daphnis shall pine
With desire, and I have no pity for him.
Make Daphnis come home now, come home now, my spells!

These keepsakes he left with me once, faithless man: 90
They are things that he wore—the most precious I own.
Mother earth, now I dig by my door and consign
Them to you—the dear keepsakes that pledge his return.
Make Daphnis come home from the city, my spells!

These simples did Moeris give me: they grow   95
By the Black Sea. I've watched him turn wolf and then fade
In the forest, raise the dead from a graveyard, and shift
A crop from one field to the next, with their aid.
Make Daphnis come home now, come home now, my spells!

Amaryllis, now carry these ashes outdoors: 100
Cast them over your shoulder—don't look when you cast—
In the river. He recks not of witchcraft or gods,
But those ashes will lead me to Daphnis at last.
Make Daphnis come home from the city, my spells!

Look! the altar is flaming, the ashes I meant
To disperse are alive—oh, miraculous fire!   105
My mind is confused, my dog barks at the gate.
Is it true, or the dream of a lover's desire?
No more spells, no more spells now—my Daphnis is near.

ECLOGA IX

LYCIDAS

Quo te, Moeri, pedes? an, quo via ducit, in urbem?

MOERIS

O Lycida, vivi pervenimus, advena nostri
(quod numquam veriti sumus) ut possessor agelli
diceret: 'haec mea sunt; veteres migrate coloni.'
nunc victi, tristes, quoniam fors omnia versat,   5
hos illi (quod nec vertat bene) mittimus haedos.

LYCIDAS

Certe equidem audieram, qua se subducere colles
incipiunt mollique iugum demittere clivo,
usque ad aquam et veteres, iam fracta cacumina, fagos—
omnia carminibus vestrum servasse Menalcan.   10

MOERIS

Audieras, et fama fuit; sed carmina tantum
nostra valent, Lycida, tela inter Martia quantum
Chaonias dicunt aquila veniente columbas.
quod nisi me quacumque novas incidere lites
ante sinistra cava monuisset ab ilice cornix,   15
nec tuus hic Moeris nec viveret ipse Menalcas.

LYCIDAS

Heu, cadit in quemquam tantum scelus? heu, tua nobis
paene simul tecum solacia rapta, Menalca?

ECLOGUE 9

LYCIDAS

Where are you footing it, Moeris? to town? this trackway
    leads there.

MOERIS

Oh, Lycidas, that I should have lived to see an outsider
Take over my little farm—a thing I had never feared—
And tell me, 'You're dispossessed, you old tenants, you've
    got to go.'
We're down and out. And look how Chance turns the tables
    on us—   5
These are *his* goats (rot them!) you see me taking to market.

LYCIDAS

Can this be true? I had heard that all the land, from the place
    where
That spur with its gentle slope sticks out from the recessive
Hill-line, as far as the water and the old beech-trees with
Their shattered tops—all this had been saved by Menalcas'
    poetry.   10

MOERIS

So you heard. That rumour did get about. But poems
Stand no more chance, where the claims of soldiers are
    involved,
Than do the prophetic doves if an eagle swoops upon them.
Indeed, but for a raven which croaked from a hollow ilex
On my left hand, and warned me to stop this last dispute   15
Whatever it cost, neither I nor Menalcas would be alive now.

LYCIDAS

Good God, what a scandalous thing this is! So we might have
    lost
Menalcas himself and the heartening pleasure his poetry gives
    us!

quis caneret Nymphas? quis humum florentibus herbis
spargeret, aut viridi fontis induceret umbra?   20
vel quae sublegi tacitus tibi carmina nuper,
cum te ad delicias ferres Amaryllida nostras?—
'Tityre, dum redeo (brevis est via) pasce capellas,
et potum pastas age, Tityre, et inter agendum
occursare capro—cornu ferit ille—caveto.'   25

MOERIS

Immo haec, quae Varo necdum perfecta canebat:
'Vare, tuum nomen, superet modo Mantua nobis,
Mantua vae miserae nimium vicina Cremonae,
cantantes sublime ferent ad sidera cycni.'

LYCIDAS

Sic tua Cyrneas fugiant examina taxos,   30
sic cytiso pastae distendant ubera vaccae,
incipe, si quid habes. et me fecere poetam
Pierides, sunt et mihi carmina, me quoque dicunt
vatem pastores; sed non ego credulus illis.
nam neque adhuc Vario videor nec dicere Cinna   35
digna, sed argutos inter strepere anser olores.

MOERIS

Id quidem ago et tacitus, Lycida, mecum ipse voluto,
si valeam meminisse; neque est ignobile carmen.
'huc ades, o Galatea; quis est nam ludus in undis?
hic ver purpureum, varios hic flumina circum   40
fundit humus flores, hic candida populus antro
imminet, et lentae texunt umbracula vites.
huc ades; insani feriant sine litora fluctus.'

Who then would have written about the nymphs, the flower-
    ing grasses
That feather the earth, and the springs thatched over with
    leaves to shade them?   20
Who would have written those lines I overheard you singing
Not long ago, on your way to our sweetheart, Amaryllis?—
Tityrus, till I return (I'm not going far), look after
My goat flock. When they have browsed, take them to water:
*   only,*
Keep away from my he-goat—a terror he is with his
*   horns.*   25

MOERIS

Why not these lines, from a poem to Varus he's not yet
    finished—
Varus, if but Mantua remains untouched—but Mantua
Stands far too close for comfort to poor Cremona—choirs of
Swans shall exalt your fame right up to the starry heavens.

LYCIDAS

Well, may your bees fly never to swarm on poisonous yew
    trees,   30
Your cows give good yields always from browsing upon the
    clover:
And so let us have some poem of your own. The Muses made
    me
A poet too. There are songs of mine. The shepherd folk
Call me their bard—though I'm not deluded by what *they* say:
I know I cannot be mentioned in the same breath with
    Cinna   35
Or Varius—a honking goose with silver-throated swans.

MOERIS

I'll try then, Lycidas. I've just been quietly searching
My memory for a poem I made—a quite good poem:—
Come to me, Galatea. What sport have you in the ocean?
Coloured spring is here. The river banks are spangled   40
With flowers of many hues. Above my grotto a silvery
Poplar sways, and vines cast a shifting lace of shadow.
Let the wild waves pound the shore, and come to me, Galatea!

LYCIDAS

Quid, quae te pura solum sub nocte canentem
audieram? numeros memini, si verba tenerem: 45
'Daphni, quid antiquos signorum suspicis ortus?
ecce Dionaei processit Caesaris astrum,
astrum quo segetes gauderent frugibus et quo
duceret apricis in collibus uva colorem.
insere, Daphni, piros: carpent tua poma nepotes.'   50

MOERIS

Omnia fert aetas, animum quoque; saepe ego longos
cantando puerum memini me condere soles:
nunc oblita mihi tot carmina; vox quoque Moerim
iam fugit ipsa: lupi Moerim videre priores.
sed tamen ista satis referet tibi saepe Menalcas.   55

LYCIDAS

Causando nostros in longum ducis amores.
et nunc omne tibi stratum silet aequor, et omnes,
aspice, ventosi ceciderunt murmuris aurae.
hinc adeo media est nobis via; namque sepulcrum
incipit apparere Bianoris. hic, ubi densas   60
agricolae stringunt frondes, hic, Moeri, canamus;
hic haedos depone, tamen veniemus in urbem.
aut si nox pluviam ne colligat ante veremur,
cantantes licet usque (minus via laedit) eamus;
cantantes ut eamus, ego hoc te fasce levabo.   65

MOERIS

Desine plura, puer, et quod nunc instat agamus:
carmina tum melius, cum venerit ipse, canemus.

LYCIDAS

And there's another—I heard you singing it all alone
One clear night. I remember its rhythm: how did the words
    go?—   45
Daphnis, why look up to old constellations rising?
Lo, the star of Olympian Caesar is in the ascendant—
A star to make our cornfields merry with bumper crops,
And warm our upland vineyards and ripen the grapes to
    purple.
Daphnis, graft your pears now: your sons' sons will enjoy
    them.   50

MOERIS

Time bears all away, even memory. In boyhood
Often I'd spend the long, long summer daylight singing.
Lost to memory, all those songs; and now my voice too
Is not what it was: the wolves ill-wished it before I could spot
    them.
Ah well, you can hear Menalcas repeat those songs when you
    like.   55

LYCIDAS

Talking thus, you have made me impatient for what I most
    want.
Look how the mere lies hushed and sleek from end to end
For you: the gusty wind has died down to silence now.
Now is the time. We're halfway along the track—I can just
Discern Bianor's tomb. So here let us stop and sing,   60
Moeris—here where labourers are thinning out the leaves.
Give your goats a rest: we shall reach town, don't worry;
Or if there's a fear the night may turn rainy, we can press on,
Singing as we go: a song lightens a long road.
Give me that pack of yours, and we'll go on our way sing-
    ing.   65

MOERIS

No, we have done enough, lad. To business! And Menalcas'
Songs will sound better still when he's home to hear us sing
    them.

ECLOGA X

Extremum hunc, Arethusa, mihi concede laborem—
pauca meo Gallo, sed quae legat ipsa Lycoris,
carmina sunt dicenda: neget quis carmina Gallo?
sic tibi, cum fluctus subterlabere Sicanos,
Doris amara suam non intermisceat undam,   5
incipe; sollicitos Galli dicamus amores,
dum tenera attondent simae virgulta capellae.
non canimus surdis, respondent omnia silvae.

    Quae nemora aut qui vos saltus habuere, puellae
Naides, indigno cum Gallus amore peribat?   10
nam neque Parnasi vobis iuga, nam neque Pindi
ulla moram fecere, neque Aonie Aganippe.
illum etiam lauri, etiam flevere myricae,
pinifer illum etiam sola sub rupe iacentem
Maenalus, et gelidi fleverunt saxa Lycaei.   15

    stant et oves circum—nostri nec paenitet illas,
nec te paeniteat pecoris, divine poeta;
et formosus ovis ad flumina pavit Adonis—
venit et upilio, tardi venere subulci,
uvidus hiberna venit de glande Menalcas.   20
omnes 'unde amor iste,' rogant, 'tibi?' venit Apollo,
'Galle, quid insanis?' inquit; 'tua cura Lycoris
perque nives alium perque horrida castra secuta est.'

ECLOGUE 10

One task, my last, I pray you to favour me in, Arethusa—
A little poem for Gallus, my friend: no one could grudge him
A poem; and may it be read by Lycoris too, his love.
Arethusa, when you stream beneath the Sicilian waters,
I wish your purity be not sullied with bitter brine: 5
And so I begin. While snub-nosed she-goats browse upon
Soft shoots, I'll tell of Gallus and the anguish of his heart.
Not to deaf ears I sing, for the woods echo my singing.
    Young Naiads, oh where were you, haunting what wood-
      land glades
Or groves, that time my Gallus was sick with hopeless
    love?   10
No duties kept you upon the ridges of Mount Parnassus
Or Pindus, or by the sacred spring at Helicon's foot.
Even the laurels, even the tamarisks wept for him
Where under a crag he lay, alone: even pine-clad Maenalus
Wept in pity for him, and the cold cliffs of Lycaeus.   15
    The sheep were standing round you—they see no shame in
      our sorrows,
So think no shame of them, my heaven-sent poet: even
Exquisite Adonis grazed sheep beside a stream.
The shepherd was there, and the swineherds heavy of gait,
    and Menalcas—
Wet he was from soaking acorns for winter mash.   20
'What fired this passion of yours?' they asked: and Apollo
    came
And said, 'You have lost your senses, Gallus. Your loved
    Lycoris
Has gone with another man, through snows and rough en-
    campments.'

venit et agresti capitis Silvanus honore,
florentis ferulas et grandia lilia quassans.   25
Pan deus Arcadiae venit, quem vidimus ipsi
sanguineis ebuli bacis minioque rubentem.
'ecquis erit modus?' inquit; 'Amor non talia curat,
nec lacrimis crudelis Amor, nec gramina rivis,
nec cytiso saturantur apes, nec fronde capellae.'   30
    tristis at ille 'tamen cantabitis, Arcades,' inquit,
'montibus haec vestris: soli cantare periti
Arcades. o mihi tum quam molliter ossa quiescant,
vestra meos olim si fistula dicat amores!
atque utinam ex vobis unus vestrique fuissem   35
aut custos gregis aut maturae vinitor uvae!
certe sive mihi Phyllis sive esset Amyntas,
seu quicumque furor—quid tum, si fuscus Amyntas?
et nigrae violae sunt et vaccinia nigra—
mecum inter salices lenta sub vite iaceret;   40
serta mihi Phyllis legeret, cantaret Amyntas.
   'hic gelidi fontes, hic mollia prata, Lycori,
hic nemus; hic ipso tecum consumerer aevo.
nunc insanus amor duri me Martis in armis
tela inter media atque adversos detinet hostis.   45
tu procul a patria—nec sit mihi credere tantum—
Alpinas a, dura, nives et frigora Rheni
me sine sola vides. a, te ne frigora laedant!
a, tibi ne teneras glacies secet aspera plantas!
   'ibo, et Chalcidico quae sunt mihi condita versu   50
carmina pastoris Siculi modulabor avena.
certum est in silvis inter spelaea ferarum,
malle pati, tenerisque meos incidere amores
arboribus: crescent illae, crescetis, amores.

Silvanus also came, in rustic coronet—flowers of
Fennel and long-stemmed lilies tossing upon his head.   25
Pan came, the god of Arcady, guised as I've often seen him,
Vermilion-stained with the juice of elderberries: he said,
Weep you no more. The Love-god has no compassion for
    sorrow.
Goats never have enough of leafage, nor bees of clover,
Nor grass of runnels; and weeping can never appease the
    Love-god.'   30
    But Gallus, sick at heart, said, 'Arcadians, you'll be singing
The tale of my love to your mountains, whatever befall. You
    are masters
Of music, you Arcadians. How tranquil my bones would rest,
If over them your reed-pipes were making my love immortal!
Ah but I wish I had been of your company, and lived
    here   35
A shepherd of your sheep or a worker in these vineyards.
Why, then I should have had a Phyllis, an Amyntas—
Some flame or other—to lie with among the sally trees
Sheltered by drooping vines. Amyntas is dark? But look at
Violets or blueberries—they have the same dusky glow.   40
Phyllis would pick me garlands, Amyntas sing for me.
    'Soft meads, cool streams you would find here, and wood-
    lands, dear Lycoris—
A paradise where we could have grown old together.
But I'm a soldier, forced by insensate zeal for the War-god
To go where weapons fly and the foe's in battle formation.   45
And you—how hard it is to believe you have left your country:
Far off among Alpine snows or over the frozen Rhine
You pass, and I'm not there. Oh may the cold not hurt you!
May splintering ice not gash your delicate feet, Lycoris!
    'But I shall go and set to music for the Sicilian   50
Shepherd's pipe the poems I wrote in Chalcidic verse.
I shall live hard in the forest, where wild beasts have their
    lairs—
My mind is made up—and cut the name of my loved Lycoris
Upon the young trees' bark: my love will grow as the trees
    grow.

interea mixtis lustrabo Maenala Nymphis,   55
aut acris venabor apros. non me ulla vetabunt
frigora Parthenios canibus circumdare saltus.
iam mihi per rupes videor lucosque sonantis
ire, libet Partho torquere Cydonia cornu
spicula—tamquam haec sit nostri medicina furoris,   60
aut deus ille malis hominum mitescere discat!
iam neque Hamadryades rursus neque carmina nobis
ipsa placent; ipsae rursus concedite silvae.
non illum nostri possunt mutare labores,
nec si frigoribus mediis Hebrumque bibamus   65
Sithoniasque nives hiemis subeamus aquosae,
nec si, cum moriens alta liber aret in ulmo,
Aethiopum versemus ovis sub sidere Cancri.
omnia vincit Amor: et nos cedamus Amori.'

    Haec sat erit, divae, vestrum cecinisse poetam,   70
dum sedet et gracili fiscellam texit hibisco,
Pierides: vos haec facietis maxima Gallo,
Gallo, cuius amor tantum mihi crescit in horas
quantum vere novo viridis se subicit alnus.
surgamus: solet esse gravis cantantibus umbra,   75
iuniperi gravis umbra, nocent et frugibus umbrae.
ite domum saturae, venit Hesperus, ite capellae.

I'll roam the slopes of Maenalus with bevies of nymphs the
    while,   55
Or hunt the vicious boar: however cold it is,
I'll whistle my hounds to cast about the Parthenian coverts.
I picture myself already, scaling the crags, halooing
Through the wide woods, letting fly with Cretan arrows there
To my heart's content.
          'As if such things could drug a frenzy like mine!   60
As if men's agonies could soften the Love-god's nature!
No, never again shall I find solace among the wood-nymphs,
Or in poetry even: words and woods mean nothing to me now.
No ordeal I could suffer would change the Love-god's heart,
Though in the deep midwinter I drank from Thracian
    streams   65
And offered myself to the sleety blizzards of Macedonia;
Or though I became a nomad shepherd beneath the searing
African sun, which scorches and kills the very elm bark.
All-conquering is Love—no use to fight against him.'

    Muses divine, may you be satisfied with these verses   70
Your poet has sung while he sat here, weaving a basket of
    slender
Marsh-mallow stems. And I pray you, make them acceptable
To Gallus, for whom my love grows greater all the time
As the green alder tree grows fast in early spring.
Now must I go. The shade of this juniper turns chill.   75
Shade stunts a crop, and it's bad for a singer's voice. My
    goats,
You have pastured well, the twilight deepens—home then,
    home!

THE GEORGICS

   . . . tot bella per orbem.
Tam multae scelerum facies, non ullus aratro
Dignus honos, squalent abductis arva colonis,
Et curvae rigidum falces conflantur in ensem.
Hinc movet Euphrates, illinc Germania bellum;
Vicinae ruptis inter se legibus urbes
Arma ferunt; saevit toto Mars impius orbe.

FOREWORD

The fascination of the Georgics for many generations of Englishmen is not difficult to explain. A century of urban civilization has not yet materially modified the instinct of a people once devoted to agriculture and stockbreeding, to the chase, to landscape gardening, to a practical love of Nature. No poem yet written has touched these subjects with more expert knowledge or more tenderness than the Georgics. In our love of domestic animals, in the millions of suburban and cottage gardens, we may see the depth and tenacity of our roots in earth to-day. It may, indeed, happen that this war, together with the spread of electrical power, will result in a decentralization of industry and the establishment of a new rural-urban civilization working through smaller social units. The factory in the fields need not remain a dream of poets and planners: it has more to commend it than the allotment in the slums.

For the translator, too, the Georgics have a special fascination. They are a work which is at once serious and charming, didactic and passionate; and didactic verse is the only kind which can be translated literally without losing the poetic quality of the original. The present translation is line for line, and literal except where a heightening of intensity in the original seemed to justify a certain freedom of interpretation.

I believe that every classical poem worth translating should be translated afresh every fifty years. The contemporary poetic idiom, whether it be derived chiefly from common speech or a literary tradition, will have changed sufficiently within that period to demand a new interpretation. To John Martyn, the Cambridge botanist, writing in 1740, Dryden's version of the Georgics already seemed to show bad taste in many passages; while to us more recent translations may appear vulgar or insipid, particularly when they are written in that peculiar kind of latin-derived pidgin-english which infects the style of so many classical scholars.

The important thing is to steer between the twin vulgarities of flashy colloquialism and perfunctory grandiloquence. This I have tried to do. I have also tried to render my translation as explicit as possible, because I made it chiefly for readers who have no Latin and because classical allusions have ceased to be commonplaces for even the highly educated. I have avoided footnotes, and attempted wherever I could to make these allusions explicit in the text (e.g. by translating 'Pales' as 'goddess of sheepfolds'). I had thought, also, of modernizing the geographical terms: but many of the places mentioned by Virgil are only doubtfully identified; the reader can be little enlightened by naming the river Strymon the river Struma, and the piling of Ossa on Pelion seems preferable to the piling of Kissovo on Plesnid.

As to the metre used here, it should be said that neither the heroic couplet nor the English hexameter—the two metres most commonly used in translations of the Georgics—seemed to me adequate now for the rendering of the Latin hexameter. After much experiment, I decided to use a rhythm based on the hexameter, containing six beats in each line, but allowing much variation of pace and interspersed with occasional short lines of three stresses. This metre, I hoped, would be elastic enough to avoid the monotony of the English hexameter, and more consonant with the speech-rhythms of the present day.

I owe many thanks to the friends whose interest in this translation encouraged me to continue with it during a time not favourable for such work: and particularly to Dr. C. M. Bowra, Warden of Wadham College, Oxford, for reading the MS. and making a number of criticisms; whatever defects of taste and scholarship remain are due solely to my own perseverance in error.

C. D. L.

June 1940

DEDICATORY STANZAS

To Stephen Spender

Poets are not in much demand these days—
We're red, it seems, or cracked, or bribed, or hearty
And, if invited, apt to spoil the party
With the oblique reproach of emigrés:
We cut no ice, although we're fancy skaters:
Aiming at art, we only strike the arty.
Poetry now, the kinder tell us, caters
For an élite: still, it gives us the hump
To think that we're the unacknowledged rump
Of a long parliament of legislators.

Where are the war poets? the fools inquire.
We were the prophets of a changeable morning
Who hoped for much but saw the clouds forewarning:
We were at war, while they still played with fire
And rigged the market for the ruin of man:
Spain was a death to us, Munich a mourning.
No wonder then if, like the pelican,
We have turned inward for our iron ration,
Tapping the vein and sole reserve of passion,
Drawing from poetry's capital what we can.

Yes, we shall fight, but—let them not mistake it—
Not for the ones who grudged to peace their pence
And gave war a blank cheque in self-defence,
Nor those who take self-interest and fake it
Into a code of honour—the distorting
Mirror those magnates hold to experience.

It's for dear life alone we shall be fighting,
The poet's living-space, the love of men,
And poets must speak for common suffering men
While history in sheets of fire is writing.

Meanwhile, what touches the heart at all, engrosses.
Through the flushed springtime and the fading year
I lived on country matters. Now June was here
Again, and brought the smell of flowering grasses
To me and death to many overseas:
They lie in the flowering sunshine, flesh once dear
To some, now parchment for the heart's release.
Soon enough each is called into the quarrel.
Till then, taking a leaf from Virgil's laurel,
I sang in time of war the arts of peace.

Virgil—a tall man, dark and countrified
In looks, they say: retiring: no rhetorician:
Of humble birth: a Celt, whose first ambition
Was to be a philosopher: Dante's guide.
But chiefly dear for his gift to understand
Earth's intricate, ordered heart, and for a vision
That saw beyond an imperial day the hand
Of man no longer armed against his fellow
But all for vine and cattle, fruit and fallow,
Subduing with love's positive force the land.

Different from his our age and myths, our toil
The same. Our exile and extravagances,
Revolt, retreat, fine faiths, disordered fancies
Are but the poet's search for a right soil
Where words may settle, marry, and conceive an
Imagined truth, for a regimen that enhances
Their natural grace. Now, as to one whom even
Our age's drought and spate have not deterred
From cherishing, like a bud of flame, the word,
I dedicate this book to you, dear Stephen.

Now, when war's long midwinter seems to freeze us
And numb our living sources once for all,
That veteran of Virgil's I recall
Who made a kitchen-garden by the Galaesus
On derelict land, and got the first of spring
From airs and buds, the first fruits in the fall,
And lived at peace there, happy as a king.
Naming him for good luck, I see man's native
Stock is perennial, and our creative
Winged seed can strike a root in anything.

LIBER I

Quid faciat laetas segetes, quo sidere terram
vertere, Maecenas, ulmisque adiungere vitis
conveniat, quae cura boum, qui cultus habendo
sit pecori, apibus quanta experientia parcis,
hinc canere incipiam. vos, o clarissima mundi   5
lumina, labentem caelo quae ducitis annum:
Liber et alma Ceres, vestro si munere tellus
Chaoniam pingui glandem mutavit arista,
poculaque inventis Acheloia miscuit uvis;
et vos, agrestum praesentia numina, Fauni—   10
ferte simul Faunique pedem Dryadesque puellae—
munera vestra cano. tuque o, cui prima frementem
fudit equum magno tellus percussa tridenti,
Neptune; et cultor nemorum, cui pinguia Ceae
ter centum nivei tondent dumeta iuvenci;   15
ipse nemus linquens patrium saltusque Lycaei
Pan, ovium custos, tua si tibi Maenala curae,
adsis, o Tegeaee, favens, oleaeque Minerva
inventrix, uncique puer monstrator aratri,
et teneram ab radice ferens, Silvane, cupressum;   20
dique deaeque omnes, studium quibus arva tueri,
quique novas alitis non ullo semine fruges,
quique satis largum caelo demittitis imbrem;
tuque adeo, quem mox quae sint habitura deorum
concilia incertum est, urbesne invisere, Caesar,   25
terrarumque velis curam, et te maximus orbis

BOOK 1

What makes the cornfields happy, under what constellation
It's best to turn the soil, my friend, and train the vine
On the elm; the care of cattle, the management of flocks,
The knowledge you need for keeping frugal bees:—all this
I'll now begin to relate. You brightest luminaries   5
Of the world, who head the year's parade across heaven's
    face:
Wine-god and kindly Harvest-goddess, if by your gift
Earth has exchanged the acorn for the rich ear of corn
And learnt to lace spring water with her discovered wine:
You Fauns, the tutelary spirits of country folk—   10
Dance here, you Fauns and Dryads—
Your bounties I celebrate. And you, Neptune, who first bade
The neighing horse start up from earth at your trident's stroke:
And you, the Forester, for whom three hundred head
Of milk-white cattle browse on the fruited bushes of Cea: 15
And you, leaving your native woods and the lawns of Arcadia,
Pan, master of flocks, if you love your Maenalus,
Come to my call and bless me: Minerva, who first discovered
The olive: the Boy who taught us the use of the crook-toothed
    plough:
Silvanus, bearing a young cypress plucked up by the
    roots:—   20
All gods and goddesses
Who care for the land, who nourish new fruits of the earth we
    sow not,
And send to our sown fields the plentiful rain from heaven.
You too, whatever place in the courts of the Immortals
Is soon to hold you—whether an overseer of cities   25
And warden of earth you'll be, Caesar, so that the great
    world

auctorem frugum tempestatumque potentem
accipiat, cingens materna tempora myrto;
an deus immensi venias maris ac tua nautae
numina sola colant, tibi serviat ultima Thule,   30
teque sibi generum Tethys emat omnibus undis:
anne novum tardis sidus te mensibus addas,
qua locus Erigonen inter Chelasque sequentis
panditur (ipse tibi iam bracchia contrahit ardens
Scorpius et caeli iusta plus parte reliquit)—   35
quidquid eris—nam te nec sperant Tartara regem
nec tibi regnandi veniat tam dira cupido,
quamvis Elysios miretur Graecia campos
nec repetita sequi curet Proserpina matrem—
da facilem cursum, atque audacibus adnue coeptis,   40
ignarosque viae mecum miseratus agrestis
ingredere et votis iam nunc adsuesce vocari.

Vere novo, gelidus canis cum montibus umor
liquitur et Zephyro putris se glaeba resolvit,
depresso incipiat iam tum mihi taurus aratro   45
ingemere, et sulco attritus splendescere vomer.
illa seges demum votis respondet avari
agricolae, bis quae solem, bis frigora sensit;
illius immensae ruperunt horrea messes.
at prius ignotum ferro quam scindimus aequor,   50
ventos et varium caeli praediscere morem
cura sit ac patrios cultusque habitusque locorum,
et quid quaeque ferat regio et quid quaeque recuset.
hic segetes, illic veniunt felicius uvae,
arborei fetus alibi, atque iniussa virescunt   55

Honour you as promoter of harvest and puissant lord
Of the seasons, garlanding your brow with your mother's
        myrtle:
Or whether you come as god of the boundless sea, and sailors
Worship your power alone, and the ends of the earth pay
        tribute,   30
And Tethys gives all her waves to get you for son-in-law:
Or whether you make a new sign in the Zodiac, where amid
        the
Slow months a gap is revealed between Virgo and Scorpio
(Already the burning Scorpion retracts his claws to leave you
More than your share of heaven):—   35
Become what you may—and Hell hopes not for you as king
And never may so ghastly a ruling ambition grip you,
Though Greece admire the Elysian Plains, and Proserpine
Care not to follow her mother who calls her back to earth—
Grant a fair passage, be gracious to this my bold design,   40
Pity with me the country people who know not the way,
Advance, and even now grow used to our invocations.

    Early spring, when a cold moisture sweats from the hoar-
        head
Hills and the brittle clods are loosening under a west wind,
Is the time for the bull to grunt as he pulls the plough deep-
        driven   45
And the ploughshare to take a shine, scoured clean in the
        furrow.
That crop, which twice has felt the sun's heat and the frost
        twice,
Will answer at last the prayers of the never-satisfied
Farmer, and burst his barns with an overflowing harvest.
But plough not an unknown plain: 50
First you must learn the winds and changeable ways of its
        weather,
The land's peculiar cultivation and character,
The different crops that different parts of it yield or yield not.
A corn-crop here, grapes there will come to the happier issue:
On another soil it is fruit trees, and grass of its own sweet
        will   55

gramina. nonne vides, croceos ut Tmolus odores,
India mittit ebur, molles sua tura Sabaei,
at Chalybes nudi ferrum, virosaque Pontus
castorea, Eliadum palmas Epirus equarum?
continuo has leges aeternaque foedera certis 60
imposuit natura locis, quo tempore primum
Deucalion vacuum lapides iactavit in orbem,
unde homines nati, durum genus. ergo age, terrae
pingue solum primis extemplo a mensibus anni
fortes invertant tauri, glaebasque iacentis 65
pulverulenta coquat maturis solibus aestas;
at si non fuerit tellus fecunda, sub ipsum
Arcturum tenui sat erit suspendere sulco:
illic, officiant laetis ne frugibus herbae,
hic, sterilem exiguus ne deserat umor harenam. 70
Alternis idem tonsas cessare novalis,
et segnem patiere situ durescere campum;
aut ibi flava seres mutato sidere farra,
unde prius laetum siliqua quassante legumen
aut tenuis fetus viciae tristisque lupini 75
sustuleris fragilis calamos silvamque sonantem.
urit enim lini campum seges, urit avenae,
urunt Lethaeo perfusa papavera somno.
sed tamen alternis facilis labor, arida tantum
ne saturare fimo pingui pudeat sola neve 80
effetos cinerem immundum iactare per agros.
sic quoque mutatis requiescunt fetibus arva,
nec nulla interea est inaratae gratia terrae.
saepe etiam sterilis incendere profuit agros,
atque levem stipulam crepitantibus urere flammis: 85
sive inde occultas viris et pabula terrae
pinguia concipiunt, sive illis omne per ignem
excoquitur vitium atque exsudat inutilis umor,
seu pluris calor ille vias et caeca relaxat

Grows green. Look you, how Tmolus gives us the saffron
    perfume,
India its ivory, the unmanly Sabaeans their incense,
The naked Chalybes iron, Pontus the rank castor,
And Elis prize-winning mares.
Nature imposed these laws, a covenant everlasting,   60
On different parts of the earth right from the earliest days
    when
Deucalion cast over a tenantless world the stones
From which arose mankind, that dour race. Now, to business:
As soon as the first months of the year begin, your strong bulls
Should turn the fertile loam and leave the clods lying   65
For the full suns of summer to bake into a fine dust:
But if the land's not heavy, you'll find it enough at the North
    Star's
Rising to ridge it out in shallow furrows:—the one
Lest weeds should check the corn's exuberance, the other
Lest lack of moisture turn your soil to a sandy desert.   70
See, too, that your arable lies fallow in due rotation,
And leave the idle field alone to recoup its strength:
Or else, changing the seasons, put down to yellow spelt
A field where before you raised the bean with its rattling
    pods
Or the small-seeded vetch   75
Or the brittle stalk and rustling haulm of the bitter lupin.
For a crop of flax burns up a field, and so does an oat-crop,
And poppies drenched in oblivion burn up its energy.
Still, by rotation of crops you lighten your labour, only
Scruple not to enrich the dried-up soil with dung   80
And scatter filthy ashes on fields that are exhausted.
So too are the fields rested by a rotation of crops,
And unploughed land in the meanwhile promises to repay
    you.
Often again it profits to burn the barren fields,
Firing their light stubble with crackling flame: uncertain   85
It is whether the earth conceives a mysterious strength
And sustenance thereby, or whether the fire burns out
Her bad humours and sweats away the unwanted moisture,
Or whether that heat opens more of the ducts and hidden

spiramenta, novas veniat qua sucus in herbas;   90
seu durat magis et venas astringit hiantis,
ne tenues pluviae rapidive potentia solis
acrior aut Boreae penetrabile frigus adurat.
multum adeo, rastris glaebas qui frangit inertis
vimineasque trahit cratis, iuvat arva, neque illum   95
flava Ceres alto nequiquam spectat Olympo;
et qui, proscisso quae suscitat aequore terga,
rursus in obliquum verso perrumpit aratro
exercetque frequens tellurem atque imperat arvis.
umida solstitia atque hiemes orate serenas,   100
agricolae; hiberno laetissima pulvere farra,
laetus ager: nullo tantum se Mysia cultu
iactat et ipsa suas mirantur Gargara messis.
quid dicam, iacto qui semine comminus arva
insequitur cumulosque ruit male pinguis harenae,   105
deinde satis fluvium inducit rivosque sequentis,
et, cum exustus ager morientibus aestuat herbis,
ecce supercilio clivosi tramitis undam
elicit? illa cadens raucum per levia murmur
saxa ciet, scatebrisque arentia temperat arva.   110
quid qui, ne gravidis procumbat culmus aristis,
luxuriem segetum tenera depascit in herba,
cum primum sulcos aequant sata, quique paludis
collectum umorem bibula deducit harena?
praesertim incertis si mensibus amnis abundans   115
exit et obducto late tenet omnia limo,
unde cavae tepido sudant umore lacunae.
Nec tamen, haec cum sint hominumque boumque labores
versando terram experti, nihil improbus anser

Pores by which her juices are conveyed to the fresh vegeta-
    tion, 90
Or rather hardens and binds her gaping veins against
Fine rain and the consuming sun's fierce potency
And the piercing cold of the north wind.
Much does he help his fields, moreover, who breaks with a
    mattock
Their lumpish clods and hauls the osier-harrow; on him 95
The golden goddess of corn looks down from heaven ap-
    proving.
He helps them too, who raises ridges along the plain
With a first ploughing, and then cross-ploughs it, constantly
Exercising the soil and mastery over his acres.
Wet midsummers and fair winters are what the farmer 100
Should ask for; in winter's powdery dust the spelt will
    flourish,
The field is in good heart: Mysia can boast no better;
Given such weather, even Gargarus is amazed by its own
    harvests.
No need to commend him who, after the sowing, closely
Follows it up by breaking the clammy loam of the field, 105
Then lets in runnels of water to irrigate the seed-land
So that, when it is fever-parched and the green blade's
    failing,
Look!—from the hilltop he coaxes the water out of its course,
And it slides over smooth pebbles whispering hoarsely and
    soothes
The parched fields with its purling. 110
Another, for fear the cornstalk should wilt under the ear's
    weight,
Grazes down the exuberant crop while yet its young green
Is barely showing above the furrows: another makes
A gravel sump to collect and drain the standing damp,
Especially if in the doubtful months the river has flooded 115
And covered the water-meadows with a wide film of mud
So that the moisture steams in a warm mist up from the
    bottoms.
Yet, though men and oxen have laboured hard on these lines
Keeping the soil turned, still can the naughty goose

Strymoniaeque grues et amaris intiba fibris 120
officiunt aut umbra nocet. pater ipse colendi
haud facilem esse viam voluit, primusque per artem
movit agros, curis acuens mortalia corda,
nec torpere gravi passus sua regna veterno.
ante Iovem nulli subigebant arva coloni; 125
ne signare quidem aut partiri limite campum
fas erat: in medium quaerebant, ipsaque tellus
omnia liberius nullo poscente ferebat.
ille malum virus serpentibus addidit atris,
praedarique lupos iussit pontumque moveri, 130
mellaque decussit foliis, ignemque removit,
et passim rivis currentia vina repressit,
ut varias usus meditando extunderet artis
paulatim, et sulcis frumenti quaereret herbam,
ut silicis venis abstrusum excuderet ignem. 135
tunc alnos primum fluvii sensere cavatas;
navita tum stellis numeros et nomina fecit—
Pleiadas, Hyadas, claramque Lycaonis Arcton;
tum laqueis captare feras et fallere visco
inventum, et magnos canibus circumdare saltus; 140
atque alius latum funda iam verberat amnem
alta petens, pelagoque alius trahit umida lina;
tum ferri rigor atque argutae lammina serrae
(nam primi cuneis scindebant fissile lignum);
tum variae venere artes. labor omnia vicit 145
improbus et duris urgens in rebus egestas.
prima Ceres ferro mortalis vertere terram
instituit, cum iam glandes atque arbuta sacrae
deficerent silvae et victum Dodona negaret.

And cranes from the river Strymon and endive's bitter
    root   120
Do damage, and shade can be harmful. For the Father of
    agriculture
Gave us a hard calling: he first decreed it an art
To work the fields, sent worries to sharpen our mortal wits
And would not allow his realm to grow listless from lethargy.
Before Jove's time no settlers brought the land under sub-
    jection;   125
Not lawful even to divide the plain with landmarks and
    boundaries:
All produce went to a common pool, and earth unprompted
Was free with all her fruits.
Jove put the wicked poison in the black serpent's tooth,
Jove told the wolf to ravin, the sea to be restive always,   130
He shook from the leaves their honey, he had all fire removed,
And stopped the wine that ran in rivers everywhere,
So thought and experiment might forge man's various crafts
Little by little, asking the furrow to yield the corn-blade,
Striking the hidden fire that lies in the veins of flint.   135
Then first did alder-trunks hollowed out take the water;
Then did the mariner group and name the stars—the Pleiads,
Hyads and the bright Bear:
Then was invented the snare for taking game, the tricky
Bird-lime, the casting of hounds about the broad wood-
    coverts.   140
One whips now the wide river with casting-net and searches
Deep pools, another trawls his dripping line in the sea.
Then came the rigid strength of steel and the shrill saw-
    blade
(For primitive man was wont to split his wood with wedges);
Then numerous arts arose. Yes, unremitting labour   145
And harsh necessity's hand will master anything.
The Corn-goddess taught men first to turn the earth with
    iron—
That was the time when acorns and arbute berries grew
    scarce
In the sacred wood, and Dodona refused them sustenance.

mox et frumentis labor additus, ut mala culmos   150
esset robigo, segnisque horreret in arvis
carduus: intereunt segetes, subit aspera silva,
lappaeque tribolique, interque nitentia culta
infelix lolium et steriles dominantur avenae.
quod nisi et adsiduis herbam insectabere rastris   155
et sonitu terrebis avis, et ruris opaci
falce premes umbram, votisque vocaveris imbrem,
heu magnum alterius frustra spectabis acervum,
concussaque famem in silvis solabere quercu.

Dicendum et quae sint duris agrestibus arma,   160
quis sine nec potuere seri nec surgere messes:
vomis et inflexi primum grave robur aratri,
tardaque Eleusinae matris volventia plaustra,
tribulaque traheaeque et iniquo pondere rastri;
virgea praeterea Celei vilisque supellex,   165
arbuteae crates et mystica vannus Iacchi.
omnia quae multo ante memor provisa repones,
si te digna manet divini gloria ruris.
continuo in silvis magna vi flexa domatur
in burim et curvi formam accipit ulmus aratri.   170
huic a stirpe pedes temo protentus in octo,
binae aures, duplici aptantur dentalia dorso:
caeditur et tilia ante iugo levis altaque fagus
stivaque, quae currus a tergo torqueat imos,
et suspensa focis explorat robora fumus.   175

Soon, too, the growing of corn became more arduous: vile
    blight   150
Attacked the stalks, and the shockheaded thistle sabotaged
    fields:
Crops fail, a prickly forest
Comes pushing up—goose-grass, star-thistle, unfeeding darnel
And barren wild-oats tyrannize over the shining tillage.
Unless you make war on the weeds relentlessly with your
    mattock   155
And scare the birds away, and pare with a bill-hook the
    darkening
Overgrowth of the country, and the rain has come to your
    call,
Vainly alas you will eye another man's heaped-up harvest
And relieve your own hunger by shaking an oak in the woods.
    I'll tell you too the armoury of the tough countryman, 160
For without this the harvest would neither be sown nor
    successful:
The ploughshare first and heavy timbers of the curving
    plough,
The ponderous-moving waggons that belong to the Mother
    of harvest,
Threshers and harrows and the immoderate weight of the
    mattock;
Slight implements, too, of osier,   165
Arbutus hurdles, the Wine-god's mystical winnowing-fan.
Be provident, lay by a stock of them long beforehand
If you wish to remain worthy of the land and its heaven-
    sent honour.
Early in woods the elm, by main force mastered, is bent
Into a share-beam and takes the shape of the curving
    plough: 170
Then to its stock are fitted a pole eight feet in length
And two earth-boards, and the share-head is set in its double
    back:
Light lime has been cut already for a yoke, and lofty beech
To make the handle that guides the whole affair from behind,
And the wood is hung up in chimneys where smoke will
    season it.   175

Possum multa tibi veterum praecepta referre,
ni refugis tenuisque piget cognoscere curas.
area cum primis ingenti aequanda cylindro
et vertenda manu et creta solidanda tenaci,
ne subeant herbae neu pulvere victa fatiscat,   180
tum variae inludant pestes: saepe exiguus mus
sub terris posuitque domos atque horrea fecit,
aut oculis capti fodere cubilia talpae,
inventusque cavis bufo et quae plurima terrae
monstra ferunt, populatque ingentem farris acervum   185
curculio atque inopi metuens formica senectae.
contemplator item, cum se nux plurima silvis
induet in florem et ramos curvabit olentis:
si superant fetus, pariter frumenta sequentur,
magnaque cum magno veniet tritura calore;   190
at si luxuria foliorum exuberat umbra,
nequiquam pinguis palea teret area culmos.
semina vidi equidem multos medicare serentis,
et nitro prius et nigra perfundere amurca,
grandior ut fetus siliquis fallacibus esset,   195
et, quamvis igni exiguo properata maderent.
vidi lecta diu et multo spectata labore
degenerare tamen, ni vis humana quotannis
maxima quaeque manu legeret. sic omnia fatis
in peius ruere ac retro sublapsa referri,   200
non aliter quam qui adverso vix flumine lembum
remigiis subigit, si bracchia forte remisit,
atque illum in praeceps prono rapit alveus amni.

Praeterea tam sunt Arcturi sidera nobis
Haedorumque dies servandi et lucidus Anguis,   205
quam quibus in patriam ventosa per aequora vectis
Pontus et ostriferi fauces temptantur Abydi.
Libra die somnique pares ubi fecerit horas,
et medium luci atque umbris iam dividit orbem,

Many the ancient saws I can relate, as long as
You're no quitter and willing to learn your modest craft.
Most urgent it is that the threshing-floor with a roller be
    flattened,
Wrought by hand, and reinforced with binding chalk,
Or else the dust may crack it and weeds come up through
    the chinks,   180
And various kinds of vermin play there: often the wee mouse
Builds underground his grange
And home, or the sightless mole scoops out his catacombs:
The toad is found in cavities, and all the manifold pests
Earth breeds; the enormous heap of spelt is spoiled by the
    weevil   185
And the ant that insures against a destitute old age.
Observe again, when the walnut clothes herself in the woods
With richest bloom and bends to earth her scented branches—
If her fruit is plentiful, a plentiful corn-crop follows,
And great will be the threshing in a season of great heat; 190
But if she is more luxuriant in shadowing leaves, you'll thresh
The corn quite fruitlessly for the straw will be full of chaff.
Many sowers indeed I have seen who doped their seed,
Bathing it first in natron or olive oil's black lees,
So the deceptive pods of the pulse might grow a bigger   195
Fruit, that should soften quickly even over a small fire.
I've noticed seed long chosen and tested with utmost care
Fall off, if each year the largest
Be not hand-picked by human toil. For a law of nature
Makes all things go to the bad, lose ground and fall away;   200
Just as an oarsman, when he is sculling his skiff against
The current, needs but relax the drive of his arms a little
And the current will carry him headlong away downstream.
    It is our task, again, to observe the star of Arcturus,
The days of the Kid, and the shining Serpent, as carefully   205
As sailors who homeward bound on windy waters are daring
The Black Sea and the straits by the oyster-beds of Abydos.
When the Scales make the hours for daytime and sleep-
    time balance,
Dividing the globe into equal hemispheres—light and dark-
    ness,

exercete, viri, tauros, serite hordea campis   210
usque sub extremum brumae intractabilis imbrem;
nec non et lini segetem et Cereale papaver
tempus humo tegere et iamdudum incumbere aratris
dum sicca tellure licet, dum nubila pendent.
vere fabis satio; tum te quoque, medica, putres   215
accipiunt sulci, et milio venit annua cura,
candidus auratis aperit cum cornibus annum
Taurus, et averso cedens Canis occidit astro.
at si triticeam in messem robustaque farra
exercebis humum, solisque instabis aristis,   220
ante tibi Eoae Atlantides abscondantur
Gnosiaque ardentis decedat stella Coronae,
debita quam sulcis committas semina, quamque
invitae properes anni spem credere terrae.
multi ante occasum Maiae coepere; sed illos   225
exspectata seges vanis elusit aristis.
si vero viciamque seres vilemque phaselum,
nec Pelusiacae curam aspernabere lentis,
haud obscura cadens mittet tibi signa Bootes:
incipe et ad medias sementem extende pruinas.   230
    Idcirco certis dimensum partibus orbem
per duodena regit mundi sol aureus astra.
quinque tenent caelum zonae: quarum una corusco
semper sole rubens et torrida semper ab igni;
quam circum extremae dextra laevaque trahuntur   235
caeruleae, glacie concretae atque imbribus atris;
has inter mediamque duae mortalibus aegris
munere concessae divum, et via secta per ambas,
obliquus qua se signorum verteret ordo.
mundus, ut ad Scythiam Riphaeasque arduus arces   240

Then set your bulls to work, farmers, and sow your
    barley   210
Up to the last showers on the frost-bound limits of winter:
The flax-plant and corn-poppy
You should cover now in earth, and keep on hard at the
    ploughing
While a bone-dry soil allows it and the weather has not yet
    broken.
In spring you sow your beans: then too the softening
    furrows   215
Will take lucerne, and millet requires its annual care;
When the milk-white Bull with gilded horn begins the year
And the Dog Star drops away.
But if for a wheat harvest or crop of hardy spelt
You work your land, and are keen on bearded corn alone,   220
Let first the Atlantid Pleiads come to their morning setting
And the blazing star of the Cretan Crown sink in the sky,
Before you commit to the furrows the seed you owe them,
    before
You entrust the hope of the year to an earth that is still
    reluctant.
Many begin to sow before the setting of Maia,   225
But empty-eared is the harvest and laughs at all their hopes.
If vetch you care to sow, or the common kidney-bean,
And if you don't look down on the care of Egyptian lentil,
Boötes setting will give you a clear signal for this:
Begin, and go on sowing up to midwinter frosts.   230
    Wherefore the golden sun commands an orbit measured
In fixed divisions through the twelvefold signs of the universe.
Five zones make up the heavens: one of them in the flaming
Sun glows red for ever, for ever seared by his fire:
Round it to right and left the furthermost zones extend,   235
Blue with cold, ice-bound, frozen with black blizzards:
Between these and the middle one, weak mortals are given
Two zones by the grace of God, and a path was cut through
    both
Where the slanting signs might march and countermarch.
    The world,
Rising steeply to Scythia and the Riphaean plateaux,   240

consurgit, premitur Libyae devexus in Austros.
hic vertex nobis semper sublimis; at illum
sub pedibus Styx atra videt Manesque profundi.
maximus hic flexu sinuoso elabitur Anguis
circum perque duas in morem fluminis Arctos,   245
Arctos Oceani metuentis aequore tingi.
illic, ut perhibent, aut intempesta silet nox,
semper et obtenta densentur nocte tenebrae;
aut redit a nobis Aurora diemque reducit,
nosque ubi primus equis Oriens adflavit anhelis,   250
illic sera rubens accendit lumina Vesper.
hinc tempestates dubio praediscere caelo
possumus, hinc messisque diem tempusque serendi,
et quando infidum remis impellere marmor
conveniat, quando armatas deducere classis,   255
aut tempestivam silvis evertere pinum.
  Nec frustra signorum obitus speculamur et ortus
temporibusque parem diversis quattuor annum.
frigidus agricolam si quando continet imber,
multa, forent quae post caelo properanda sereno,   260
maturare datur: durum procudit arator
vomeris obtunsi dentem, cavat arbore lintres,
aut pecori signum aut numeros impressit acervis.
exacuunt alii vallos furcasque bicornis,
atque Amerina parant lentae retinacula viti.   265
nunc facilis rubea texatur fiscina virga,
nunc torrete igni fruges, nunc frangite saxo.
quippe etiam festis quaedam exercere diebus
fas et iura sinunt: rivos deducere nulla

Slopes down in the south to Libya.

This North pole's always above us: the South appears beneath
The feet of darkling Styx, of the deep-down Shadow People.
Here the great Snake glides out with weaving, elastic body
Writhing riverwise around and between the two Bears—　245
The Bears that are afraid to get wet in the water of Ocean.
At the South pole, men say, either it's dead of night,
Dead still, the shadows shrouded in night, blacked out for
　　ever;
Or dawn returns from us thither, bringing the daylight back,
And when sunrise salutes us with the breath of his panting
　　horses,　　　　　　　　　　　　　　　　　250
Down there eve's crimson star is lighting his lamp at last.
Hence we foreknow the weather of the uncertain sky,
The time to reap or sow,
The time that's best for lashing the treacherous sea with oars
And launching an armed fleet,　　　　　　　　255
The proper time to throw the pine tree in the forest.

　　Well for us that we watch the rise and fall of the sky-
　　　signs
And the four different seasons that divide the year equally.
Suppose the farmer is kept indoors by a spell of cold rain,
He can take his time about many jobs which later he'd have
　　to　　　　　　　　　　　　　　　　　　260
Scamp when the weather cleared: the ploughman hammers
　　the hard tooth
Of the blunt plough: one chap will fashion troughs from a
　　tree-trunk,
Another brand his cattle or number his sacks of grain.
Some sharpen stakes and forks,
Get ready ties of willow to bind the trailing vine.　　265
Now you may weave light baskets from shoots of the bramble
　　bush,
Dry your corn at the fire now and grind it down with a
　　millstone.
Even on festival days some labours are allowed
By the laws of god and man: no religious scruple need stop
　　you

religio vetuit, segeti praetendere saepem,   270
insidias avibus moliri, incendere vepres,
balantumque gregem fluvio mersare salubri.
saepe oleo tardi costas agitator aselli
vilibus aut onerat pomis, lapidemque revertens
incusum aut atrae massam picis urbe reportat.   275
    Ipsa dies alios alio dedit ordine Luna
felicis operum. quintam fuge: pallidus Orcus
Eumenidesque satae; tum partu Terra nefando
Coeumque Iapetumque creat saevumque Typhoea
et coniuratos caelum rescindere fratres.   280
ter sunt conati imponere Pelio Ossam
scilicet, atque Ossae frondosum involvere Olympum;
ter pater exstructos disiecit fulmine montis.
septima post decimam felix et ponere vitem
et prensos domitare boves et licia telae   285
addere. nona fugae melior, contraria furtis.
    Multa adeo gelida melius se nocte dedere,
aut cum sole novo terras inrorat Eous.
nocte leves melius stipulae, nocte arida prata
tondentur, noctes lentus non deficit umor.   290
et quidam seros hiberni ad luminis ignis
pervigilat, ferroque faces inspicat acuto;
interea longum cantu solata laborem
arguto coniunx percurrit pectine telas,
aut dulcis musti Volcano decoquit umorem   295
et foliis undam trepidi despumat aëni.
at rubicunda Ceres medio succiditur aestu,
et medio tostas aestu terit area fruges.

From works of irrigation or hedging around your corn-
     field,   270
Bird-snaring, firing the brambles,
Dipping your bleating flock of sheep in the wholesome
     river.
Often its driver loads the flanks of the dawdling ass
With oil or with cheap apples, and returns from town later
Bearing a whetstone ready dressed or a lump of black
     pitch.   275
  The moon herself has made some days in varying degrees
Lucky for work. Beware of the fifth: that is the birthday
Of Hell's pale king and the Furies; then earth spawned an
     unspeakable
Brood of titans and giants, gave birth to the ogre Typhoeus
And the brothers who leagued themselves to hack the heavens
     down: 280
Three times they tried, three times, to pile Ossa on Pelion—
Yes, and to roll up leafy Olympus on Ossa's summit;
And thrice our Father dislodged the heaped-up hills with a
     thunderbolt.
The seventeenth day is lucky both for setting a vine,
Roping and breaking steers, and fixing the loops on a
     loom.   285
The ninth is a good day for runaways, bad for burglars.
  Many things even go best in the raw night-hours or at sun-
     rise
When the Dawn Star dews the earth.
By night it's best to mow light stubble, by night a meadow
That's parched, for a clammy moisture is always present
     at night-time.   290
A man there is who stays up late by winter firelight
With a penknife pointing torches;
Meanwhile, singing a song to lighten the lengthy task,
His wife runs through the loom with her shrill-rattling reed,
Or boils away on a fire the sweet liquid of wine-must   295
And skims with leaves the wave that foams in the shud-
     dering kettle.
But the red-gold corn should always be cut in noonday heat,
In noonday heat the baked grain beat out on threshing-floor.

nudus ara, sere nudus. hiems ignava colono:
frigoribus parto agricolae plerumque fruuntur,   300
mutuaque inter se laeti convivia curant.
invitat genialis hiems curasque resolvit;
ceu pressae cum iam portum tetigere carinae,
puppibus et laeti nautae imposuere coronas.
sed tamen et quernas glandes tum stringere tempus   305
et lauri bacas oleamque cruentaque myrta:
tum gruibus pedicas et retia ponere cervis,
auritosque sequi lepores, tum figere dammas
stuppea torquentem Balearis verbera fundae,
cum nix alta iacet, glaciem cum flumina trudunt.   310
    Quid tempestates autumni et sidera dicam,
atque, ubi iam breviorque dies et mollior aestas,
quae vigilanda viris? vel cum ruit imbriferum ver,
spicea iam campis cum messis inhorruit et cum
frumenta in viridi stipula lactentia turgent?   315
saepe ego, cum flavis messorem induceret arvis
agricola et fragili iam stringeret hordea culmo,
omnia ventorum consurgere proelia vidi,
quae gravidam late segetem ab radicibus imis
sublimem expulsam eruerent: ita turbine nigro   320
ferret hiems culmumque levem stipulasque volantis.
saepe etiam immensum caelo venit agmen aquarum
et foedam glomerant tempestatem imbribus atris
collectae ex alto nubes; ruit arduus aether,
et pluvia ingenti sata laeta boumque labores   325
diluit; implentur fossae et cava flumina crescunt
cum sonitu fervetque fretis spirantibus aequor.
ipse Pater media nimborum in nocte corusca
fulmina molitur dextra: quo maxima motu

Plough and sow in the warm months, in your shirt-sleeves.
    Winter's an off-time
For farmers: then they mostly enjoy their gains, hold
    jolly   300
Suppers amongst themselves.
Genial winter invites them and they forget their worries;
Just as, when ships in cargo have come to port at last,
Glad to be home the sailors adorn their poops with garlands.
Yet even now there's employment in season—acorns to
    gather   305
And berries off the bay tree, and olives, and blood-red myrtle:
Now you can lay your traps for the crane, your nets for the
    stag,
Go coursing long-eared hares, or whirl your hempen sling
To bring the fallow deer down—
Now when snow lies deep and streams jostle their pack-
    ice.   310
    Am I to tell you next of the storms and stars of autumn?
The things, when days draw in and summer's heat is abating,
That men must guard against? The dangers of showery spring,
When the prick-eared harvest already bristles along the plains
And when in the green blade the milky grain is swelling?   315
Well, often I've seen a farmer lead into his golden fields
The reapers and begin to cut the frail-stalked barley,
And winds arise that moment, starting a free-for-all,
Tearing up by the roots whole swathes of heavy corn
And hurling them high in the air: with gusts black as a
    hurricane   320
The storm sent flimsy blades and stubble flying before it.
Often, too, huge columns of water come in the sky
And clouds charged off the deep amass for dirty weather
With rain-squalls black: then the whole sky gives way, falls,
Floods with terrific rain the fertile crops and the labours   325
Of oxen; filled are the ditches, dry rivers arise in spate
Roaring, the sea foams and seethes up the hissing fjords.
The Father, enthroned in midnight cloud, hurls from a
    flashing
Right hand his lightning: the whole

terra tremit; fugere ferae et mortalia corda   330
per gentis humilis stravit pavor: ille flagranti
aut Athon aut Rhodopen aut alta Ceraunia telo
deicit; ingeminant Austri et densissimus imber:
nunc nemora ingenti vento, nunc litora plangunt.
hoc metuens caeli mensis et sidera serva,   335
frigida Saturni sese quo stella receptet
quos ignis caeli Cyllenius erret in orbis.
in primis venerare deos, atque annua magnae
sacra refer Cereri laetis operatus in herbis
extremae sub casum hiemis, iam vere sereno.   340
tum pingues agni et tum mollissima vina,
tum somni dulces densaeque in montibus umbrae.
cuncta tibi Cererem pubes agrestis adoret:
cui tu lacte favos et miti dilue Baccho,
terque novas circum felix eat hostia fruges,   345
omnis quam chorus et socii comitentur ovantes,
et Cererem clamore vocent in tecta; neque ante
falcem maturis quisquam supponat aristis
quam Cereri torta redimitus tempora quercu
det motus incompositos et carmina dicat.   350
   Atque haec ut certis possemus discere signis,
aestusque pluviasque et agentis frigora ventos,
ipse pater statuit quid menstrua luna moneret,
quo signo caderent Austri, quid saepe videntes
agricolae propius stabulis armenta tenerent.   355
continuo ventis surgentibus aut freta ponti
incipiunt agitata tumescere et aridus altis
montibus audiri fragor, aut resonantia longe

Earth trembles at the shock; the beasts are fled, and human   330
Hearts are felled in panic throughout the nations: on Athos,
Rhodope or the Ceraunian massif his bolt flares down:
The south wind doubles its force and thicker falls the rain:
Now wail the woods with that gale tremendous, now the shores wail.

Fearing this, keep track of the signs and constellations,   335
Notice whither the cold star of Saturn takes himself
And into what sky-circles Mercury is moving.
Above all, worship the gods, paying your yearly tribute
To the Corn-goddess—a sacrifice on the cheerful grass
Just at the close of winter, when spring has cleared the sky.   340
Oh then the lambs are fat, then are wines most mellow,
Sweet then is sleep and rich on mountains lie the shadows.
Let all your labouring men worship the Corn-goddess:
For her let the honeycomb be steeped in milk and mild wine,
The mascot led three times round the young crops—a victim   345
Fêted by all your fellows accompanying it in a body:
Let them call her into their houses
With a shout, and let nobody lay his sickle to the ripe corn
Till in her honour he's placed on his head a wreath of oak leaves
And danced impromptu dances and sung the harvester's hymn.   350

  So that we might be able to predict from manifest signs
These things—heatwaves and rain and winds that bring cold weather,
The Father himself laid down what the moon's phases should mean,
The cue for the south wind's dropping, the sign that often noted
Should warn a farmer to keep his cattle nearer the shippon.   355
At once, when winds are rising,
The sea begins to fret and heave, and a harsh crackling
Is heard from timbered heights, or a noise that carries far

litora misceri et nemorum increbrescere murmur.
iam sibi tum curvis male temperat unda carinis,   360
cum medio celeres revolant ex aequore mergi
clamoremque ferunt ad litora, cumque marinae
in sicco ludunt fulicae, notasque paludes
deserit atque altam supra volat ardea nubem.
saepe etiam stellas vento impendente videbis   365
praecipitis caelo labi, noctisque per umbram
flammarum longos a tergo albescere tractus;
saepe levem paleam et frondes volitare caducas,
aut summa nantis in aqua conludere plumas.
at Boreae de parte trucis cum fulminat, et cum   370
Eurique Zephyrique tonat domus, omnia plenis
rura natant fossis atque omnis navita ponto
umida vela legit. numquam imprudentibus imber
obfuit: aut illum surgentem vallibus imis
aëriae fugere grues, aut bucula caelum   375
suspiciens patulis captavit naribus auras,
aut arguta lacus circumvolitavit hirundo
et veterem in limo ranae cecinere querelam.
saepius et tectis penetralibus extulit ova
angustum formica terens iter, et bibit ingens   380
arcus, et e pastu decedens agmine magno
corvorum increpuit densis exercitus alis.
iam variae pelagi volucres et quae Asia circum
dulcibus in stagnis rimantur prata Caystri,
certatim largos umeris infundere rores,   385
nunc caput obiectare fretis, nunc currere in undas
et studio incassum videas gestire lavandi.

Comes confused from the beaches, and copses moan cre-
    scendo.
At such a time are the waves in no temper to bear your
    curved ship—   360
A time when gulls are blown back off the deepsea flying
Swift and screeching inland, a time when cormorants
Play on dry land, and the heron
Leaves his haunt in the fens to flap high over the cloud.
Another gale-warning often is given by shooting stars   365
That streak downsky and blaze a trail through the night's
    blackness
Leaving a long white wake:
Often light chaff and fallen leaves eddy in the air,
Or feathers play tig skimming along the skin of water.
But when lightning appears from the quarter of the grim
    north wind,   370
When it thunders to south or west, then all the countryside
Is a-swim with flooded dykes and all the sailors at sea
Close-reef their dripping sails. No, rain need never take us
Unawares: for high-flying cranes will have flown to valley
    bottoms
To escape the rain as it rises, or else a calf has looked up   375
At the sky and snuffed the wind with nostrils apprehensive,
Or the tittering swallow has flitted around and around the
    lake,
And frogs in the mud have croaked away at their old com-
    plaint.
Often too from her underground workings the emmet,
    wearing
A narrow path, bears out her eggs; a giant rainbow   380
Bends down to drink; rook armies desert their feeding-
    ground
In a long column, wing-tip to wing-tip, their wings whirring.
Now seabirds after their kind, and birds that about Caÿster's
Asian waterflats grub in the fresh pools, zestfully fling
Showers of spray over their shoulders,   385
Now ducking their heads in the creeks, scampering now at
    the wavelets,
Making a bustle and frivolous pantomime of washing.

tum cornix plena pluviam vocat improba voce
et sola in sicca secum spatiatur harena.
ne nocturna quidem carpentes pensa puellae   390
nescivere hiemem, testa cum ardente viderent
scintillare oleum et putris concrescere fungos.

   Nec minus ex imbri soles et aperta serena
prospicere et certis poteris cognoscere signis:
nam neque tum stellis acies obtunsa videtur,   395
nec fratris radiis obnoxia surgere Luna,
tenuia nec lanae per caelum vellera ferri;
non tepidum ad solem pennas in litore pandunt
dilectae Thetidi alcyones, non ore solutos
immundi meminere sues iactare maniplos.   400
at nebulae magis ima petunt campoque recumbunt,
solis et occasum servans de culmine summo
nequiquam seros exercet noctua cantus.
apparet liquido sublimis in aëre Nisus,
et pro purpureo poenas dat Scylla capillo: 405
quacumque illa levem fugiens secat aethera pennis,
ecce inimicus atrox magno stridore per auras
insequitur Nisus; qua se fert Nisus ad auras,
illa levem fugiens raptim secat aethera pennis.
tum liquidas corvi presso ter gutture voces   410
aut quater ingeminant, et saepe cubilibus altis
nescio qua praeter solitum dulcedine laeti
inter se in foliis strepitant: iuvat imbribus actis
progeniem parvam dulcisque revisere nidos.
haud equidem credo, quia sit divinitus illis   415
ingenium aut rerum fato prudentia maior;
verum, ubi tempestas et caeli mobilis umor
mutavere vias et Iuppiter uvidus Austris

Then the truculent raven full-throated announces rain
As she stalks alone on the dry sand.
Even at night can girls, spinning their wool, be aware   390
That a storm approaches, for then they behold in the burning
      lamp
The oil sputter and crumbly mould collect on the wick.
  No less easy it is to foretell after rainy weather
Sun and unclouded skies, and by sure indications to know
      them.
Then, neither do star rays look blurred nor will the moon
      rise   395
As though she owed her light to the beams of her brother sun,
Nor lank and fleecy clouds be drawn across the heaven:
Kingfishers then, the pets of the Sea-goddess, will not preen
      their
Plumage along the shore in the warm sun, nor will gross
Swine remember to root and toss with their snouts the bed-
      straw.   400
Rather do mists hang low and crouch along the plain,
And the little owl, perched on a gable, watching the sun go
      down,
Keeps at her crazy night-call.
Aloft in the lucid air Nisus, a sparrowhawk,
Appears, and Scylla pays for that purple hair she stole: 405
Wherever in flight she parts the thin air with her lark's wing,
Look! her enemy, cruel, down the wind loudly whistling,
Nisus follows her close; where Nisus zooms upwind,
Frantic in flight she parts the thin air with her lark's wing.
Then rooks, the guttural talkers, three times or four
      repeat   410
A clear cool note, and often up there in the treetop cradles
Charmed by some unfamiliar sweet impulse we cannot guess
      at
Gossip among the leaves: they love, when rain is over,
To visit again their baby brood, their darling nests.
It's not, to my belief, that God has given them   415
A special instinct, or Fate a wider foreknowledge of things;
But, when the weather's changing, when the wet atmosphere
Shifts and a sky dripping from the south wind condenses

denset, erant quae rara modo, et quae densa relaxat,
vertuntur species animorum, et pectora motus   420
nunc alios, alios dum nubila ventus agebat,
concipiunt: hinc ille avium concentus in agris
et laetae pecudes et ovantes gutture corvi.

Si vero solem ad rapidum lunasque sequentis
ordine respicies, numquam te crastina fallet   425
hora, neque insidiis noctis capiere serenae.
luna revertentis cum primum colligit ignis,
si nigrum obscuro comprenderit aëra cornu,
maximus agricolis pelagoque parabitur imber;
at si virgineum suffuderit ore ruborem,   430
ventus erit: vento semper rubet aurea Phoebe.
sin ortu quarto (namque is certissimus auctor)
pura neque obtunsis per caelum cornibus ibit,
totus et ille dies et qui nascentur ab illo
exactum ad mensem pluvia ventisque carebunt,   435
votaque servati solvent in litore nautae
Glauco et Panopeae et Inoo Melicertae.
sol quoque et exoriens et cum se condet in undas
signa dabit; solem certissima signa sequuntur,
et quae mane refert et quae surgentibus astris.   440
ille ubi nascentem maculis variaverit ortum
conditus in nubem medioque refugerit orbe,
suspecti tibi sint imbres; namque urget ab alto
arboribusque satisque Notus pecorique sinister.
aut ubi sub lucem densa inter nubila sese   445
diversi rumpent radii, aut ubi pallida surget
Tithoni croceum linquens Aurora cubile,
heu, male tum mitis defendet pampinus uvas;
tam multa in tectis crepitans salit horrida grando.
hoc etiam, emenso cum iam decedit Olympo,   450

What was rare just now and rarefies what was condensed,
New images possess their mind, impulses move 420
Their heart other than moved them while the wind was
  herding the clouds.
Thus, the countryside over, begins that bird-chorale,
Beasts rejoice, and rooks caw in their exultation.

  If you observe the hotfoot sun and the moon's phases,
To-morrow will never cheat you 425
Nor will you be taken in by the trick of a cloudless night.
When first at the new moon her radiance is returning,
If she should clasp a dark mist within her unclear crescent,
Heavy rain is in store for farmer and fisherman:
But if a virgin blush covers her face, there'll be 430
Some wind—wind always flushes the face of the golden moon.
And if at her fourth rising (this is a sign infallible)
She walk the heaven in purity of light, her horns not blurred,
All that day and the days
Which follow to the month's end you'll fear no rain or
  wind, 435
And sailors ashore shall pay their vows for a safe return to
Glaucus and Panope and Melicertes son of Ino.
The sun also at dawning and when he sinks in the deep
Will give you signs: his signs are the most reliable of all,
Both those he brings in the morning and those at the stars'
  ascending. 440
When at dawn he's dappled
With spots, concealed behind cloud, and half his orb is
  hidden,
You may look out for showers; for a southerly gale off the sea
Is driving, that means no good to trees or crops or cattle.
But when, towards daybreak, his beams filter between 445
Thick cloud, rayed out like spokes, or when the dawn arises
Pale from the saffron bed of Tithonus, then I fear
Vine-leaves will give your ripening grapes but poor protec-
  tion—
Such a storm of harsh hail is coming to rattle and bounce on
  the roofs.
This too, when he's traversed the sky and is now declin-
  ing, 450

profuerit meminisse magis; nam saepe videmus
ipsius in vultu varios errare colores:
caeruleus pluviam denuntiat, igneus Euros;
sin maculae incipient rutilo immiscerier igni,
omnia tum pariter vento nimbisque videbis   455
fervere. non illa quisquam me nocte per altum
ire neque ab terra moveat convellere funem.
at si, cum referetque diem condetque relatum,
lucidus orbis erit, frustra terrebere nimbis,
et claro silvas cernes Aquilone moveri.   460
denique, quid vesper serus vehat, unde serenas
ventus agat nubes, quid cogitet umidus Auster,
sol tibi signa dabit. solem quis dicere falsum
audeat? ille etiam caecos instare tumultus
saepe monet fraudemque et operta tumescere bella. 465
ille etiam exstincto miseratus Caesare Romam,
cum caput obscura nitidum ferrugine texit
impiaque aeternam timuerunt saecula noctem.
tempore quamquam illo tellus quoque et aequora ponti,
obscenaeque canes importunaeque volucres   470
signa dabant. quotiens Cyclopum effervere in agros
vidimus undantem ruptis fornacibus Aetnam,
flammarumque globos liquefactaque volvere saxa!
armorum sonitum toto Germania caelo
audiit, insolitis tremuerunt motibus Alpes.   475
vox quoque per lucos vulgo exaudita silentis
ingens, et simulacra modis pallentia miris
visa sub obscurum noctis, pecudesque locutae—
(infandum!). sistunt amnes terraeque dehiscunt,
et maestum inlacrimat templis ebur aeraque sudant. 480
proluit insano contorquens vertice silvas

Is of even more advantage to remember:—we often see
Various colours passing over his countenance;
The dark-green stands for rain, flame colour foretells an east
    wind;
But, should stains begin to be mixed with a ruddy fire,
Both wind and rain are brewing and you'll see them boiling
    over.   455
No one on such a night
Could induce me to cross the sea or even cast off my moorings.
But if, when he brings a dayspring and when he buries that
    day,
His orb is equally clear, you need not worry for rain-clouds,
Since you'll be watching the forests wave in a fine north
    wind.   460
Lastly, what the late evening conveys, from whence the wind
    drives
Fine-weather clouds, and what the damp south wind is
    brooding,
The sun discloses. Who dares call the sun a liar?
Often too he warns you of lurking imminent violence,
Of treachery, and wars that grow in the dark like a
    cancer.   465
The sun, when Caesar fell, had sympathy for Rome—
That day he hid the brightness of his head in a rusty fog
And an evil age was afraid his night would last for ever:
Though at that time the earth as well, the waves of the sea,
Mongrels and birds morose   470
Gave tongue to the doom. How often we saw Mount Aetna
    deluge
The fields of the Cyclops with lava from her cracked furnaces,
Rolling up great balls of flame and molten rocks!
In Germany they heard a clash of fighting echo
Through the whole sky: the Alps shook with unnatural
    shudders.   475
Likewise in stilly woods a voice was heard by many—
A monster voice, and phantoms miraculously pale
Were met at the dusk of night, and cattle spoke—an omen
Unspeakable! Rivers stopped, earth gaped, and ivories
In temples wept sad tears and brazen images sweated.   480
Po, the king of rivers, in maniac spate whirled round

fluviorum rex Eridanus, camposque per omnis
cum stabulis armenta tulit. nec tempore eodem
tristibus aut extis fibrae apparere minaces
aut puteis manare cruor cessavit, et altae   485
per noctem resonare lupis ululantibus urbes.
non alias caelo ceciderunt plura sereno
fulgura, nec diri totiens arsere cometae.
ergo inter sese paribus concurrere telis
Romanas acies iterum videre Philippi;   490
nec fuit indignum superis bis sanguine nostro
Emathiam et latos Haemi pinguescere campos.
   scilicet et tempus veniet cum finibus illis
agricola incurvo terram molitus aratro
exesa inveniet scabra robigine pila,   495
aut gravibus rastris galeas pulsabit inanis,
grandiaque effossis mirabitur ossa sepulcris.
di patrii, Indigetes, et Romule Vestaque mater,
quae Tuscum Tiberim et Romana Palatia servas,
hunc saltem everso iuvenem succurrere saeclo   500
ne prohibete. satis iam pridem sanguine nostro
Laomedonteae luimus periuria Troiae.
iam pridem nobis caeli te regia, Caesar,
invidet, atque hominum queritur curare triumphos,
quippe ubi fas versum atque nefas; tot bella per orbem,   505
tam multae scelerum facies, non ullus aratro
dignus honos, squalent abductis arva colonis,
et curvae rigidum falces conflantur in ensem.
hinc movet Euphrates, illinc Germania bellum;
vicinae ruptis inter se legibus urbes   510
arma ferunt; saevit toto Mars impius orbe:
ut cum carceribus sese effudere quadrigae,
addunt in spatia, et frustra retinacula tendens
fertur equis auriga, neque audit currus habenas.

Forests, washed them away, swept all over the plains
Herds and their byres together. A time it was when the guts of
Woe-working victims never failed to reveal the worst
Nor wells to seep with blood   485
Nor high-built cities to sound all night with the wolves'
          howling.
Never elsewhere have lightnings flickered so constantly
In a clear sky, or baleful comets burned so often.
Thus it ensued that Philippi's field saw Roman armies
Once again engaged in the shock of civil war;   490
And the High Ones did not think it a shame that we should
          twice
Enrich with our blood Emathia and the broad plains of
          Haemus.
     Surely the time will come when a farmer on those frontiers
Forcing through earth his curved plough
Shall find old spears eaten away with flaky rust,   495
Or hit upon helmets as he wields the weight of his mattock
And marvel at the heroic bones he has disinterred.
O Gods of our fathers, native Gods, Romulus, Vesta
Who mothers our Tuscan Tiber and the Roman Palatine,
At least allow our young prince to rescue this shipwrecked
          era!   500
Long enough now have we
Paid in our blood for the promise Laomedon broke at Troy.
Long now has the court of heaven grudged you to us, Caesar,
Complaining because you care only for mortal triumphs.
For Right and Wrong are confused here, there's so much war
          in the world,   505
Evil has so many faces, the plough so little
Honour, the labourers are taken, the fields untended,
And the curving sickle is beaten into the sword that yields not.
There the East is in arms, here Germany marches:
Neighbour cities, breaking their treaties, attack each
          other: 510
The wicked War-god runs amok through all the world.
So, when racing chariots have rushed from the starting-gate,
They gather speed on the course, and the driver tugs at the
          curb-rein
—His horses runaway, car out of control, quite helpless.

LIBER II

Hactenus arvorum cultus et sidera caeli:
nunc te, Bacche, canam, nec non silvestria tecum
virgulta et prolem tarde crescentis olivae.
huc, pater o Lenaee—tuis hic omnia plena
muneribus, tibi pampineo gravidus autumno   5
floret ager, spumat plenis vindemia labris—
huc, pater o Lenaee, veni, nudataque musto
tinge novo mecum dereptis crura coturnis.
    Principio arboribus varia est natura creandis.
namque aliae nullis hominum cogentibus ipsae   10
sponte sua veniunt camposque et flumina late
curva tenent, ut molle siler lentaeque genistae,
populus et glauca canentia fronde salicta;
pars autem posito surgunt de semine, ut altae
castaneae, nemorumque Iovi quae maxima frondet   15
aesculus, atque habitae Grais oracula quercus.
pullulat ab radice aliis densissima silva,
ut cerasis ulmisque: etiam Parnasia laurus
parva sub ingenti matris se subicit umbra.
hos natura modos primum dedit, his genus omne   20
silvarum fruticumque viret nemorumque sacrorum.
sunt alii, quos ipse via sibi repperit usus.
hic plantas tenero abscindens de corpore matrum
deposuit sulcis: hic stirpes obruit arvo

BOOK 2

So far I have sung the tillage of earth, the lore of heaven:
Now it's the turn of wine, and with it the trees that crowd
In woody copse, and the produce of the gradual-growing
    olive.
Come, Lord of the wine-press—everything here is lavish
By your largesse, for you the field's aflower and laden   5
With bines of autumn, the vintage foams in vats overflowing—
Come then, Lord of the wine-press, pull off your boots and
    paddle
Bare-legged with me and dye your shins purple in the grape
    juice!
    To begin. Nature is catholic in the propagation of trees.
Some without human help   10
Spring of their own sweet will and spread abroad by winding
Streams and on plains—soft osier, the bending Spanish broom,
Poplars, and the pale willow that shows a silver-blue leaf:
Again, some grow from seed they have dropped—the high-
    tiered chestnut,
The common oak, most prolific of leaf among woodland
    trees,   15
And the oak that in Greece they fancy is able to tell their
    fortune.
Others, like elm and cherry, have a thick undergrowth
Cropping up from their roots: the Parnassian bay-tree also,
When tiny, shelters beneath the immense shade of its mother.
Nature gave from the start such modes to evolve the green
    of   20
Each tribe of trees in forest, shrubbery, sacred wood.
Others we've found by experience.
One man takes suckers off the tender stock of the mother
And plants them in trenches: another fixes sets in the field

quadrifidasque sudes et acuto robore vallos.   25
silvarumque aliae pressos propaginis arcus
exspectant et viva sua plantaria terra.
nil radicis egent aliae, summumque putator
haud dubitat terrae referens mandare cacumen.
quin et caudicibus sectis—mirabile dictu—   30
truditur e sicco radix oleagina ligno.
et saepe alterius ramos impune videmus
vertere in alterius, mutatamque insita mala
ferre pirum, et prunis lapidosa rubescere corna.

　　Quare agite o proprios generatim discite cultus,   35
agricolae, fructusque feros mollite colendo,
neu segnes iaceant terrae. iuvat Ismara Baccho
conserere atque olea magnum vestire Taburnum.
tuque ades, inceptumque una decurre laborem,
o decus, o famae merito pars maxima nostrae,   40
Maecenas, pelagoque volans da vela patenti.
non ego cuncta meis amplecti versibus opto,
non, mihi si linguae centum sint oraque centum,
ferrea vox. ades et primi lege litoris oram;
in manibus terrae: non hic te carmine ficto   45
atque per ambages et longa exorsa tenebo.

　　Sponte sua quae se tollunt in luminis oras,
infecunda quidem, sed laeta et fortia surgunt;
quippe solo natura subest. tamen haec quoque, si quis
inserat aut scrobibus mandet mutata subactis,   50
exuerint silvestrem animum, cultuque frequenti
in quascumque voles artis haud tarda sequentur.
nec non et sterilis quae stirpibus exit ab imis,
hoc faciet, vacuos si sit digesta per agros:
nunc altae frondes et rami matris opacant   55
crescentique adimunt fetus uruntque ferentem.
iam quae seminibus iactis se sustulit arbos,
tarda venit, seris factura nepotibus umbram,

By notching stakes cross-wise or sharpening the wood to a
    point.   25
Some forest trees there are prefer the pinned-down arches
Of the layer, that make a nursery alive in the parent's earth.
Some need no root, and the pruner
Can safely commit to the soil cuttings from off a high branch.
What's more—and this is a marvel—if you take a saw to the
    trunk of   30
An olive, a root will come pushing out from the dry wood.
Often again we observe the boughs of one tree change
Without harm into another's—grafted apples growing
On a pear, and stony cherries reddening upon a plum tree.
   So come, you countrymen, learn the correct training of
    each   35
In its kind, domesticate wild fruits by your cultivation,
And let not the earth be lazy! It's good to plant with vines
Ismarus, and to clothe in olives Mount Taburnus.
And you, be at hand, and help me complete the task I've
    begun—
My pride, who rightfully share the chief of my renown—   40
My friend, and unfurl your flying sails for the sea lies open.
I cannot hope to include everything in my poem,
No, not if I'd a hundred tongues, a hundred mouths
And a voice like iron. But come and coast the shore: dry land
Is near: I'll not detain you   45
With lengthy preambles, digressions, or any poetic fiction.
   Trees that spontaneously reach up to the world of light
Bear no fruit, it's true, but they grow up bonny and strong,
For natural vigour is in their soil. Yet even these, if
You graft on them or transplant them into prepared
    trenches,   50
Will cast their wildwood ways, and by constant cultivation
Be disciplined soon to whatever habits you design for them.
Even a barren sucker that shoots from the bottom of a tree
Will do the same, if you plant it out in open ground:
Otherwise, the leaves and boughs of its mother blanket it   55
From above, stifle its growth, dry up its fruitfulness.
A tree that springs from dropped seed
Grows slowly, it'll give shade one day to your descendants:

pomaque degenerant sucos oblita priores,
et turpis avibus praedam fert uva racemos.   60
scilicet omnibus est labor impendendus, et omnes
cogendae in sulcum ac multa mercede domandae.
sed truncis oleae melius, propagine vites
respondent, solido Paphiae de robore myrtus;
plantis et durae coryli nascuntur et ingens   65
fraxinus Herculeaeque arbos umbrosa coronae,
Chaoniique patris glandes; etiam ardua palma
nascitur et casus abies visura marinos.
inseritur vero et fetu nucis arbutus horrida,
et steriles platani malos gessere valentis,   70
castaneae fagos, ornusque incanuit albo
flore piri, glandemque sues fregere sub ulmis.
   Nec modus inserere atque oculos imponere simplex.
nam qua se medio trudunt de cortice gemmae
et tenuis rumpunt tunicas, angustus in ipso   75
fit nodo sinus; huc aliena ex arbore germen
includunt udoque docent inolescere libro.
aut rursum enodes trunci resecantur, et alte
finditur in solidum cuneis via, deinde feraces
plantae immittuntur: nec longum tempus, et ingens   80
exiit ad caelum ramis felicibus arbos,
miraturque novas frondes et non sua poma.
   Praeterea genus haud unum nec fortibus ulmis
nec salici lotoque nec Idaeis cyparissis,
nec pingues unam in faciem nascuntur olivae,   85
orchades et radii et amara pausia baca,
pomaque et Alcinoi silvae, nec surculus idem
Crustumiis Syriisque piris gravibusque volaemis.
non eadem arboribus pendet vindemia nostris
quam Methymnaeo carpit de palmite Lesbos;   90

Apples deteriorate, losing their pristine savour,
And the vine bears nasty grapes that are good for nothing but
    birds.   60
The fact is, all of these require attention, all
Must be forced into furrows and tamed with much expense
    of labour.
Olives will answer best to truncheons, vines to the layer,
Myrtles to solid sets:
From slips you propagate the hardwood hazel, the huge   65
Ash, the shady poplar—the crown of Hercules,
And Jupiter's oaks; so too the palm that scales the sky
Is reared, and the fir that goes to take its chance at sea.
But the rugged arbutus is ingrafted from off the walnut,
And barren planes have carried a hearty crop of apples,   70
Chestnuts have borne beech-mast, the mountain ash blown
    white
With pear blossom, and pigs munched acorns under an elm
    tree.
  Grafting and budding are two different operations.
Where buds push out from the bark
And burst their delicate sheaths, you should make a narrow
    slit   75
In the actual knot: it's here that you enclose a bud
From another tree and train it to grow in the sappy rind.
Grafting's different—it's done by cutting a smooth trunk,
Splitting the wood deeply with wedges, and then inserting
The fertile scion: before long   80
That tree ascends to heaven in a wealth of happy branches,
Surprised at its changeling leaves and the fruits that are not
    its own.
  Next, there's more than a single species of hardy elms,
Of the willow, the nettle tree, or the cypresses of Ida;
More than one variety of fat olives you'll find—   85
Orchites, the raggaria, and the bitter-berried posea:
Many sorts of apples there are in orchards; the same branch
Bears not the Crustumine pear, the bergamot and the pound-
    pear.
Different the vintage grapes that trail on our own trees
From those you gather in Lesbos off a Methymnian vine.   90

sunt Thasiae vites, sunt et Mareotides albae,
pinguibus hae terris habiles, levioribus illae,
et passo Psithia utilior tenuisque Lageos
temptatura pedes olim vincturaque linguam,
purpureae preciaeque, et quo te carmine dicam   95
Raetica? nec cellis ideo contende Falernis.
sunt et Aminneae vites, firmissima vina,
Tmolius adsurgit quibus et rex ipse Phanaeus
Argitisque minor, cui non certaverit ulla
aut tantum fluere aut totidem durare per annos.   100
non ego te, dis et mensis accepta secundis,
transierim, Rhodia, et tumidis, Bumaste, racemis.
sed neque quam multae species nec nomina quae sint
est numerus: neque enim numero comprendere refert;
quem qui scire velit, Libyci velit aequoris idem   105
discere quam multae Zephyro turbentur harenae,
aut ubi navigiis violentior incidit Eurus
nosse quot Ionii veniant ad litora fluctus.
    Nec vero terrae ferre omnes omnia possunt.
fluminibus salices crassisque paludibus alni   110
nascuntur, steriles saxosis montibus orni;
litora myrtetis laetissima; denique apertos
Bacchus amat collis, Aquilonem et frigora taxi.
aspice et extremis domitum cultoribus orbem
Eoasque domos Arabum pictosque Gelonos: 115
divisae arboribus patriae. sola India nigrum
fert hebenum, solis est turea virga Sabaeis.
quid tibi odorato referam sudantia ligno
balsamaque et bacas semper frondentis acanthi?
quid nemora Aethiopum molli canentia lana,   120
velleraque ut foliis depectant tenuia Seres?
aut quos Oceano propior gerit India lucos,

Thasian and white Mareotic

Vines there are, one suited to heavy soil, one to light soil;

Psythian are best for raisin wine, while thin Lagean

On its day will trip your feet and tie your tongue in a knot.

There's the purple grape and the early. What poem can do
  justice   95

To Rhaetian? Yet even this cannot compete with Falernian.

Amminean vines afford us the most full-bodied wine,

To which must yield the Tmolian and even the royal Chian

And lesser Argite—though none other can rival the latter

For sheer abundance or length of time it remains at its
  best.   100

I'm not forgetting Rhodian wine, by gods and festive

Mortals highly esteemed, or the bountiful grapes of Bumastus.

But to catalogue all the wines and their names would be quite
  beyond me

And serve no useful purpose:

If you wish to know their number, go and tot up the
  grains   105

Of sand that are whirled around by a sand-storm in the
  Sahara,

Or count the waves that break along Adriatic coasts

When an easterly gale comes down in gusts upon the
  shipping.

 Now different plants will need different soils for their
  nurture.

Willows grow by streams, alders in soggy marshland; 110

The barren rowan tree is found on rocky hillsides;

Myrtles crowd to the sea-coast:

Vines love an open hill, yews a cold northerly aspect.

Consider the ends of the earth and those who cultivate them—

Arabs away in the east, Ukrainians in their woad: 115

No less widespread are the homes of trees. India alone

Gives ebony, Arabia the tree of frankincense.

Need I tell you about the balsam that distils

From fragrant wood, or the globes of evergreen gum-arabic?

The soft cotton that glimmers in plantations of Ethiopia? 120

The way the Chinese comb the delicate silk from their leaves?

Then there's the Indian jungle that borders Ocean, just

extremi sinus orbis, ubi aëra vincere summum
arboris haud ullae iactu potuere sagittae—
et gens illa quidem sumptis non tarda pharetris?   125
Media fert tristis sucos tardumque saporem
felicis mali, quo non praesentius ullum,
pocula si quando saevae infecere novercae
miscueruntque herbas et non innoxia verba,
auxilium venit ac membris agit atra venena.   130
ipsa ingens arbos faciemque simillima lauro;
et, si non alium late iactaret odorem,
laurus erat: folia haud ullis labentia ventis;
flos ad prima tenax; animas et olentia Medi
ora fovent illo et senibus medicantur anhelis.   135
   Sed neque Medorum silvae, ditissima terra,
nec pulcher Ganges atque auro turbidus Hermus
laudibus Italiae certent, non Bactra neque Indi
totaque turiferis Panchaia pinguis harenis.
haec loca non tauri spirantes naribus ignem   140
invertere satis immanis dentibus hydri,
nec galeis densisque virum seges horruit hastis;
sed gravidae fruges et Bacchi Massicus umor
implevere; tenent oleae armentaque laeta.
hinc bellator equus campo sese arduus infert,   145
hinc albi, Clitumne, greges et maxima taurus
victima, saepe tuo perfusi flumine sacro,
Romanos ad templa deum duxere triumphos.
hic ver adsiduum atque alienis mensibus aestas:
bis gravidae pecudes, bis pomis utilis arbos.   150
at rabidae tigres absunt et saeva leonum
semina, nec miseros fallunt aconita legentis,
nec rapit immensos orbis per humum neque tanto
squameus in spiram tractu se colligit anguis.
adde tot egregias urbes operumque laborem,   155

In the furthest corner of the world: no arrow can reach its
    tree-tops
However hard they shoot—and the Indians, I assure you,
Aren't fools at archery.   125
Persia gives us the peart juice and the lingering taste
Of citron, a favoured fruit, and one that will come in handy
If ever an unkind stepmother puts anything in your cup—
Poisonous herbs, for instance, mixed with malignant cantrips—
As an antidote to drive the toxin out of your system.   130
The tree itself is big, very like a bay in appearance:
Indeed, were it not for the different perfume it wafts abroad,
A bay it was: the leaves won't fall in any wind,
The flower is most tenacious: this tree is used by the Medes
To sweeten a stinking breath and to cure old men of
    asthma.   135
    But neither the Median forests, that rich land, nor fair
    Ganges.
Nor Hermus rolling in gold
√ Compares with Italy—no, not Bactra nor the Indies
Nor all Arabia's acres of spice-enrichened soil.
This land of ours has never been ploughed by bulls fire-
    breathing   140
Nor sown with dragon's teeth;
It has never known a harvest of serried helmeted spearmen:
Rather is it a country fulfilled with heavy corn and
Campanian wine, possessed by olives and prosperous herds.
Here the charger gallops onto the plain in his pride,   145
Here the white-fleeced flocks and the bull, a princely victim
Washed over and over in Clitumnus' holy water,
Head our Roman triumphs to the temples of the gods.
Here is continual spring and a summer beyond her season;
Cattle bear twice yearly, apples a second crop.   150
No bloodthirsty tigers are found here, no fierce young lions
    roar,
No monkshood grows to deceive and poison the wretch who
    picks it,
Nor does the scaly snake slither at such great length
On the ground or gather himself into so many coils here.
Number our noble cities and all the works of our hands,   155

tot congesta manu praeruptis oppida saxis
fluminaque antiquos subterlabentia muros.
an mare quod supra memorem, quodque adluit infra?
anne lacus tantos? te, Lari maxime, teque,
fluctibus et fremitu adsurgens Benace marino?   160
an memorem portus Lucrinoque addita claustra
atque indignatum magnis stridoribus aequor,
Iulia qua ponto longe sonat unda refuso
Tyrrhenusque fretis immittitur aestus Avernis?
haec eadem argenti rivos aerisque metalla   165
ostendit venis atque auro plurima fluxit.
haec genus acre virum, Marsos pubemque Sabellam,
adsuetumque malo Ligurem, Volscosque verutos
extulit; haec Decios, Marios, magnosque Camillos,
Scipiadas duros bello, et te, maxime Caesar,   170
qui nunc extremis Asiae iam victor in oris
imbellem avertis Romanis arcibus Indum.
salve, magna parens frugum, Saturnia tellus,
magna virum: tibi res antiquae laudis et artis
ingredior, sanctos ausus recludere fontis,   175
Ascraeumque cano Romana per oppida carmen.
   Nunc locus arvorum ingeniis, quae robora cuique,
quis color, et quae sit rebus natura ferendis.
difficiles primum terrae collesque maligni,
tenuis ubi argilla et dumosis calculus arvis,   180
Palladia gaudent silva vivacis olivae.
indicio est tractu surgens oleaster eodem
plurimus et strati bacis silvestribus agri.
at quae pinguis humus dulcique uligine laeta,
quique frequens herbis et fertilis ubere campus,   185
qualem saepe cava montis convalle solemus
despicere (huc summis liquuntur rupibus amnes
felicemque trahunt limum), quique editus Austro

The towns piled up on toppling cliffs, the antique walls
And the rivers that glide below them.
Must I commemorate the Upper sea and the Lower?
The lakes so great? Lake Larius the greatest of them all,
Lake Benacus that tosses and growls like a little ocean?   160
Shall I mention our harbours, the mole that was built to bar
     the Lucrine
And made the deep cry out in mighty indignation
Where the Sound of Julius murmurs with the noise of the sea
     locked out
And Tyrrhene tides flow through a canal into Averno?
Veins of silver and copper Italy too has revealed   165
And rivers running with gold.
Active her breed of men—the Marsians and Sabellians,
Ligurians used to hardship, Volscian javelin-throwers;
Mother she is of the Decii, Marii, great Camilli,
The Scipio's relentless in war; and of you, most royal
     Caesar,   170
Who now triumphant along the furthest Asian frontiers
Keep the war-worthless Indians away from the towers of
     Rome.
Hail, great mother of harvests! O land of Saturn, hail!
Mother of men! For you I take my stand on our ancient
Glories and arts, I dare to unseal the hallowed sources   175
And sing a rural theme throughout the cities of Rome.
     Now it is time to deal with the nature of different soils,
The strength and colour of each, their quotient of fertility.
First, a stubborn soil and inhospitable hills,
Where the clay is lean and the fields are strewn with stones
     and brushwood,   180
Delight in the long-lived olive.
You'll know such soil by the wealth of wild olives that grow
All over it and litter the ground with their wild berries.
But where the soil is rich and rejoices in sweet moisture,
Or a level expanse grown deep with grass all lush and
     verdant,   185
Such as we often find when we look down into a fold
Of the hollow hills (for becks flow hither bearing alluvial
Soil from the heights above), or an upland facing south

et filicem curvis invisam pascit aratris:
hic tibi praevalidas olim multoque fluentis 190
sufficiet Baccho vitis, hic fertilis uvae,
hic laticis, qualem pateris libamus et auro,
inflavit cum pinguis ebur Tyrrhenus ad aras,
lancibus et pandis fumantia reddimus exta.

sin armenta magis studium vitulosque tueri, 195
aut ovium fetum aut urentis culta capellas,
saltus et saturi petito longinqua Tarenti,
et qualem infelix amisit Mantua campum
pascentem niveos herboso flumine cycnos:
non liquidi gregibus fontes, non gramina deerunt, 200
et quantum longis carpent armenta diebus
exigua tantum gelidus ros nocte reponet.

nigra fere et presso pinguis sub vomere terra,
et cui putre solum (namque hoc imitamur arando)
optima frumentis: non ullo ex aequore cernes 205
plura domum tardis decedere plaustra iuvencis.
aut unde iratus silvam devexit arator
et nemora evertit multos ignava per annos,
antiquasque domos avium cum stirpibus imis
eruit; illae altum nidis petiere relictis, 210
at rudis enituit impulso vomere campus.
nam ieiuna quidem clivosi glarea ruris
vix humilis apibus casias roremque ministrat;
et tofus scaber et nigris exesa chelydris
creta negant alios aeque serpentibus agros 215
dulcem ferre cibum et curvas praebere latebras.

Where the plough is baulked by bracken:—
Such sites as these one day will produce superlative
    vines,   190
Robust and in wine abundant; generous givers of the grape
And of that juice we pour to the gods from a golden chalice
While the plump Etruscan plays his ivory flute at the altar
And platters bend with the weight of the smoking sacrifice.
    But if your business be rather the keeping of calves and
    cattle,   195
The breeding of sheep, or goats that burn up all growing
    things,
You should try the woodland pastures and the prairies of rich
    Tarentum
And plains such as unlucky Mantua has lost
Where snow-white swans among the river weeds are feeding:
Here neither springs of water nor grass will fail your
    flocks,   200
And all that the cattle consume
In a long day is restored by the cool dew during the short
    night.
    As a rule, soil that is black and turns up rich at the pressure
Of the ploughshare, or crumbling soil (for this we reproduce
By ploughing) is best for corn: no other plain will yield
    you   205
So many waggonloads drawn home by the slow-gait oxen.
Or acres from which the ploughman has carted the wood
    away:
Intolerant of trees that stood idle for many a year,
He felled them, root and branch he demolished the ancient
    dwellings
Of birds; their nests abandoned, the birds have made for the
    sky,   210
But the land that once was wild is gleaming now with furrows.
In hill-country you'll get gravel, a hungry soil
That gives the bees a bare subsistence of spurge and rose-
    mary:
Friable stone and chalk is where the black snakes burrow
Finding no land its like   215
For dainty food and the tunnelling of their serpentine retreats.

quae tenuem exhalat nebulam fumosque volucris,
et bibit umorem et, cum vult, ex se ipsa remittit,
quaeque suo semper viridi se gramine vestit,
nec scabie et salsa laedit robigine ferrum,   220
illa tibi laetis intexet vitibus ulmos,
illa ferax oleo est, illam experiere colendo
et facilem pecori et patientem vomeris unci.
talem dives arat Capua et vicina Vesevo
ora iugo et vacuis Clanius non aequus Acerris.   225
   Nunc quo quamque modo possis cognoscere dicam.
rara sit an supra morem si densa requires
(altera frumentis quoniam favet, altera Baccho—
densa magis Cereri, rarissima quaeque Lyaeo),
ante locum capies oculis alteque iubebis   230
in solido puteum demitti, omnemque repones
rursus humum et pedibus summas aequabis harenas.
si deerunt, rarum pecorique et vitibus almis
aptius uber erit; sin in sua posse negabunt
ire loca et scrobibus superabit terra repletis,   235
spissus ager; glaebas cunctantis crassaque terga
exspecta et validis terram proscinde iuvencis.
salsa autem tellus et quae perhibetur amara
(frugibus infelix ea, nec mansuescit arando,
nec Baccho genus aut pomis sua nomina servat)   240
tale dabit specimen: tu spisso vimine qualos
colaque prelorum fumosis deripe tectis;
huc ager ille malus dulcesque a fontibus undae
ad plenum calcentur: aqua eluctabitur omnis
scilicet et grandes ibunt per vimina guttae;   245
at sapor indicium faciet manifestus et ora
tristia temptantum sensu torquebit amaro.

Land that is breathing out lank mist and volatile vapours,
That drinks the moisture up or sweats it away at will
And wears an evergreen garment made of its own grasses
And does not affect your implements with salty, scurfy
　　　rust—　　　　　　　　　　　　　　　　　　　　220
That land will prove a winner at winding your elms with vines
And yielding olive oil: just try that land and you'll find it
A masterpiece for grazing, a meek one for the plough.
Such land they farm round Capua, in the country beside
　　　Vesuvius,
And where the floods of the Clanius have emptied old
　　　Acerrae.　　　　　　　　　　　　　　　　　　225
　　Now let me tell you how to distinguish the various soils.
If you wish to know whether soil is loose or uncommonly stiff
(For corn requires the one and vineyards thrive on the other—
Compact soil suiting the former, a loose-knit one the latter),
First mark a place with your eye and have a pit sunk
　　　deep　　　　　　　　　　　　　　　　　　　　230
In the solid ground, then put all the earth back again
And stamp it level on top:
If it fails to fill up the cavity, that soil is loose and fitted
For pasture and generous vines: but if you cannot replace
It all, and earth is left over after you've filled the pit,　235
That land is of close texture; look out for clinging clods there—
A sticky glebe that'll need your strongest oxen to plough it.
Salty land, again, and land as they say that is 'sour'
(No catch for corn, to be sweetened by no amount of
　　　ploughing,
Where vines lose quality and orchards their reputation)　240
You'll detect by this experiment:—take down from your
　　　smoky rafters
Baskets of plaited withies and the strainers used in a wine-
　　　press;
Fill them up with that nasty soil and fresh spring-water
And tread them well together:
The water will all strain off in large drops through the
　　　withies,　　　　　　　　　　　　　　　　　　245
But the bitter taste of it will show as plain as a pikestaff
On the face of the taster, twisting it into a sour grimace.

pinguis item quae sit tellus hoc denique pacto
discimus: haud umquam manibus iactata fatiscit,
sed picis in morem ad digitos lentescit habendo.   250
umida maiores herbas alit, ipsaque iusto
laetior. a, nimium ne sit mihi fertilis illa,
nec se praevalidam primis ostendat aristis!
quae gravis est ipso tacitam se pondere prodit,
quaeque levis. promptum est oculis praediscere nigram,   255
et quis cui color. at sceleratum exquirere frigus
difficile est: piceae tantum taxique nocentes
interdum aut hederae pandunt vestigia nigrae.

His animadversis terram multo ante memento
excoquere et magnos scrobibus concidere montis,   260
ante supinatas Aquiloni ostendere glaebas,
quam laetum infodias vitis genus. optima putri
arva solo: id venti curant gelidaeque pruinae
et labefacta movens robustus iugera fossor.
at si quos haud ulla viros vigilantia fugit,   265
ante locum similem exquirunt, ubi prima paretur
arboribus seges et quo mox digesta feratur,
mutatam ignorent subito ne semina matrem.
quin etiam caeli regionem in cortice signant,
ut, quo quaeque modo steterit, qua parte calores   270
austrinos tulerit, quae terga obverterit axi,
restituant: adeo in teneris consuescere multum est.

collibus an plano melius sit ponere vitem
quaere prius. si pinguis agros metabere campi,
densa sere: in denso non segnior ubere Bacchus.   275
sin tumulis acclive solum collisque supinos,
indulge ordinibus; nec setius omnis in unguem
arboribus positis secto via limite quadret:

Further, soil that is fat and rich will answer briefly
To the following test: when tossed in the hand it never crumbles
But adheres to the fingers, like pitch growing stickier in the handling.   250
Damp ground encourages rank vegetation; by nature it runs
To freakish growth. Preserve me from land that is over-fertile
And proves itself too strong by a precocious corn-crop!
Weigh the soil in your hand and it gives you a quiet hint
Whether it's light or heavy: you'll learn at a glance that it's black   255
Or whatever colour it may be. But to find the damnable cold soil
Is difficult: only Corsican pines and poisonous yew trees
At times betray it, or sprawling ivy offers a clue.

Bearing in mind these rules, remember to give your land
Plenty of sun, and trench the broad hillsides, and turn   260
Your clods to welcome the north wind,
Long before you plant your vines. Best are the fields
Where soil is crumbly: winds and hard frosts take care of that,
And a deal of hard digging to stir and loosen the acres.
But if a man intends to take extra precaution,   265
He'll choose a similar soil both for his seedlings' nursery
And for the vineyard where they are soon to be planted out,
Lest the young slips find their foster-mother unsympathetic.
What's more, he may even carve on the bark four points of the compass
So that, when a plant is transferred, it shall turn the same face   270
To north or south as it turned
From birth: so important are habits developed in early days.
Find out first if your vines are better laid out upon
Hilly or level ground. When you're plotting out rich plain-land,
Sow thickly: a thick-set vineyard is no more backward in bearing.   275
On ground that is broken by tumps and on the recumbent hills
Give your rows more elbow-room; but see that the alleys
Of trees are planted there in squares with equal precision:

ut saepe ingenti bello cum longa cohortis
explicuit legio et campo stetit agmen aperto,   280
derectaeque acies, ac late fluctuat omnis
aere renidenti tellus, necdum horrida miscent
proelia, sed dubius mediis Mars errat in armis.
omnia sint paribus numeris dimensa viarum;
non animum modo uti pascat prospectus inanem,   285
sed quia non aliter viris dabit omnibus aequas
terra, neque in vacuum poterunt se extendere rami.
    Forsitan et scrobibus quae sint fastigia quaeras.
ausim vel tenui vitem committere sulco.
altior ac penitus terrae defigitur arbos,   290
aesculus in primis, quae quantum vertice ad auras
aetherias tantum radice in Tartara tendit.
ergo non hiemes illam, non flabra neque imbres
convellunt; immota manet multosque nepotes,
multa virum volvens durando saecula vincit.   295
tum fortis late ramos et bracchia tendens
huc illuc media ipsa ingentem sustinet umbram.
    Neve tibi ad solem vergant vineta cadentem,
neve inter vitis corylum sere; neve flagella
summa pete aut summa defringe ex arbore plantas   300
(tantus amor terrae), neu ferro laede retunso
semina, neve oleae silvestris insere truncos:
nam saepe incautis pastoribus excidit ignis,
qui furtim pingui primum sub cortice tectus
robora comprendit, frondesque elapsus in altas   305
ingentem caelo sonitum dedit; inde secutus
per ramos victor perque alta cacumina regnat,

Just as in war when a legion deploys by companies
From column of route into line across an open plain,   280
And the ranks are dressed by the right, and the earth all
     undulates
With flashing bronze, and the battle
Waits while the War-god saunters uncertain between the
     armies.
Let all be spaced out in alleys of perfect symmetry,
Not merely so that their vistas may charm a frivolous
     mind,   285
But because only thus can earth supply impartial
Vigour to all, and the growing boughs have room to extend.
     You will ask me perhaps what depth you ought to dig your
     trenches.
The vine I'd venture to plant in quite a shallow one:
But trees should be set deeper, well down in the earth's
     heart—   290
The oak above all, that raises
Her head as far into heaven as her roots go down towards hell:
Wherefore no storms, no gusts, no rains can ever uproot her,
But immovable she remains
Outlasting children's children through centuries of human
     life.   295
Far and wide she stretches her boughs, her steadfast arms—
A central column upholding that heavy spread of shade.
     Avoid sloping your vineyard towards the setting sun,
And planting hazel among the vines. Never take the highest
Vine-shoots, nor tear your cuttings from off the top of a
     tree   300
(Such is earth's attraction, the lower do best), nor with blunt
     blade
Wound the young vines. Don't plant wild olive to support
     your vines:
For often it happens some careless shepherd lets fall a spark
That, smouldering furtively under their resinous bark at first,
Gets a grip on the wood, leaps out on the leaves aloft,   305
And roars at the sky; rears up then
In triumph over the branches and crests of the trees, their
     master,

et totum involvit flammis nemus et ruit atram
ad caelum picea crassus caligine nubem,
praesertim si tempestas a vertice silvis   310
incubuit, glomeratque ferens incendia ventus.
hoc ubi, non a stirpe valent caesaeque reverti
possunt atque ima similes revirescere terra;
infelix superat foliis oleaster amaris.

  Nec tibi tam prudens quisquam persuadeat auctor   315
tellurem Borea rigidam spirante movere.
rura gelu tunc claudit hiems, nec semine iacto
terrae patitur radicem adfigere concretam.
optima vinetis satio cum vere rubente
candida venit avis longis invisa colubris,   320
prima vel autumni sub frigora, cum rapidus Sol
nondum hiemem contingit equis, iam praeterit aestas.
ver adeo frondi nemorum, ver utile silvis,
vere tument terrae et genitalia semina poscunt.
tum pater omnipotens fecundis imbribus Aether   325
coniugis in gremium laetae descendit, et omnis
magnus alit magno commixtus corpore fetus.
avia tum resonant avibus virgulta canoris,
et Venerem certis repetunt armenta diebus;
parturit almus ager, Zephyrique trementibus auris   330
laxant arva sinus; superat tener omnibus umor;
inque novos soles audent se gramina tuto
credere, nec metuit surgentis pampinus Austros
aut actum caelo magnis Aquilonibus imbrem,
sed trudit gemmas et frondes explicat omnis.   335
non alios prima nascentis origine mundi
inluxisse dies aliumve habuisse tenorem
crediderim: ver illud erat, ver magnus agebat
orbis, et hibernis parcebant flatibus Euri,

Rolling the whole plantation in flame, heavenward heaving
A cloud of smoke gross-bodied, greasy and black as pitch—
And worse still if a storm bears down on the wood to
    marshal   310
The flames and fan them afar. Should this befall, your vines
Are dead to the roots; you may cut them away, but they'll not
    recover
Nor awake in green from the earth below as once they did:
Wild olives alone will live there, a barren, bitter stock.
    Let no one, however canny, induce you to work your
    land   315
When it's bone-hard under a north wind.
Then icy winter closes down the countryside—
You may cast your seed, but the numb root will never take
    hold on earth.
The time for setting vines is the first flush of spring
When that white bird arrives, the stork, the bane of ser-
    pents;   320
Or the first frosts of autumn, days when the hotfoot sun
Is not on winter's verge yet, but summer is now passing.
Oh, spring is good for leaves in the spinney, good to forests,
In spring the swelling earth aches for the seed of new life.
Then the omnipotent Father of air in fruitful showers   325
Comes down to his happy consort
And greatly breeds upon her great body manifold fruit.
Then are the trackless copses alive with the trilling of birds,
And the beasts look for love, their hour come round again:
Lovely the earth in labour, under a tremulous west wind   330
The fields unbosom, a mild moisture is everywhere.
Confident grows the grass, for the young sun will not harm it;
The shoots of the vine are not scared of a southerly gale arising
Or the sleety rain that slants from heaven beneath a north
    wind,—
No, bravely now they bud and all their leaves display.   335
So it was, I believe, when the world first began,
Such the illustrious dawning and tenor of their days.
It was springtime then, great spring
Enhanced the earth and spared it the bitter breath of an east
    wind—

cum primae lucem pecudes hausere, virumque   340
terrea progenies duris caput extulit arvis,
immissaeque ferae silvis et sidera caelo.
nec res hunc tenerae possent perferre laborem,
si non tanta quies iret frigusque caloremque
inter, et exciperet caeli indulgentia terras.   345

Quod superest, quaecumque premes virgulta per agros,
sparge fimo pingui et multa memor occule terra,
aut lapidem bibulum aut squalentis infode conchas;
inter enim labentur aquae, tenuisque subibit
halitus, atque animos tollent sata. iamque reperti   350
qui saxo super atque ingentis pondere testae
urgerent: hoc effusos munimen ad imbris,
hoc ubi hiulca siti findit Canis aestifer arva.

Seminibus positis superest diducere terram
saepius ad capita et duros iactare bidentis,   355
aut presso exercere solum sub vomere et ipsa
flectere luctantis inter vineta iuvencos;
tum levis calamos et rasae hastilia virgae
fraxineasque aptare sudes furcasque valentis,
viribus eniti quarum et contemnere ventos   360
adsuescant summasque sequi tabulata per ulmos.

Ac dum prima novis adolescit frondibus aetas,
parcendum teneris, et dum se laetus ad auras
palmes agit laxis per purum immissus habenis,
ipsa acie nondum falcis temptanda, sed uncis   365
carpendae manibus frondes interque legendae.
inde ubi iam validis amplexae stirpibus ulmos
exierint, tum stringe comas, tum bracchia tonde:
ante reformidant ferrum; tum denique dura

A time when the first cattle lapped up the light, and men   340
Children of earth themselves arose from the raw champaign,
And wild things issued forth in the wood, and stars in the sky.
How could so delicate creatures endure the toil they must,
Unless between cold and heat there came this temperate spell
And heaven held the earth in his arms and comforted
     her?   345
   To proceed: whatever plantations you're setting down on
     your land,
Spread rich dung and be careful to cover with plenty of earth:
Dig in some porous stones or rough shells at their roots
Through which the rain-water may trickle and evaporate
     again
And the plants perk up their spirits.   350
Men have been known ere now to lay a rock above them
Or a weighty potsherd—protection against a flooding rain,
When heatwave comes with the Dog Star and cracks the
     fields with thirst.
   Once you have set the seedlings, it remains to loosen the
     soil
Thoroughly at their roots, and ply the heavy hoe;   355
To discipline the soil with deep-pressed plough, and steer
Your straining oxen up and down the alleys of the vineyard.
Then make ready and fit smooth reeds, poles of peeled wood,
Ash stakes for the forked uprights,
Upon whose strength your vines can mount and be trained to
     clamber   360
Up the high-storied elm trees, not caring tuppence for wind.
   As long as your vines are growing in first and infant leaf,
They're delicate, need indulgence. And while the gay shoots
     venture
Heavenward, given their head and allowed to roam the sky,
Don't use a knife upon them yet—a fingernail   365
Is enough for pruning their leaves and thinning them out in
     places.
But when they've shot up and are holding the elms in strong
     embrace,
Dock the leaves, lop the branches:
Till now they could not bear the steel; now you must show
     them

exerce imperia et ramos compesce fluentis.   370
  Texendae saepes etiam et pecus omne tenendum,
praecipue dum frons tenera imprudensque laborum;
cui super indignas hiemes solemque potentem
silvestres uri adsidue capreaeque sequaces
inludunt, pascuntur oves avidaeque iuvencae.   375
frigora nec tantum cana concreta pruina
aut gravis incumbens scopulis arentibus aestas
quantum illi nocuere greges durique venenum
dentis et admorsu signata in stirpe cicatrix.
non aliam ob culpam Baccho caper omnibus aris   380
caeditur, et veteres ineunt proscaenia ludi,
praemiaque ingeniis pagos et compita circum
Thesidae posuere, atque inter pocula laeti
mollibus in pratis unctos saluere per utres.
nec non Ausonii, Troia gens missa, coloni   385
versibus incomptis ludunt risuque soluto,
oraque corticibus sumunt horrenda cavatis,
et te, Bacche, vocant per carmina laeta, tibique
oscilla ex alta suspendunt mollia pinu.
hinc omnis largo pubescit vinea fetu,   390
complentur vallesque cavae saltusque profundi
et quocumque deus circum caput egit honestum.
ergo rite suum Baccho dicemus honorem
carminibus patriis, lancesque et liba feremus,
et ductus cornu stabit sacer hircus ad aram,   395
pinguiaque in veribus torrebimus exta colurnis.
  Est etiam ille labor curandis vitibus alter,
cui numquam exhausti satis est: namque omne quotannis
terque quaterque solum scindendum glaebaque versis
aeternum frangenda bidentibus, omne levandum   400

Greater severity, curbing their frisky wanton growth.   370
  There's hedging, too, to be done: every kind of beast you
      must bar,
Especially while the vine-leaf is young and inexperienced.
For, beside cruel winters and bullying suns, the woodland
Buffalo and restless hunting roedeer habitually
Make a playground there, and sheep and greedy heifers a
      pasture.   375
White frosts that stiffen all
And heat of summer that lies so heavy on scorching crags
Hurt a vineyard less than flocks with their venomous teeth
And the scars they leave on the nibbled stems will damage it.
This accounts for the sacrifice of a goat to the Wine-god   380
On every altar, the staging of the ancient ritual plays,
The prizes that round their hamlets and crossroads the
      Athenians
Gave for local talent, when they danced on the greasy wine-
      skins
Junketing in the meadows and jolly in their cups.
The Ausonians, too, settlers from Troy, are accustomed to
      hold a   385
Beano, their poems unpolished and unrestrained their jokes:
They wear the most hideous wooden
Masks, and address the Wine-god in jovial ditties, and hang
Wee images of the god to sway from windy pine-boughs.
Thus will every vine advance to full fruition   390
And valleys will teem and dells and dingles and combes
      deep-wooded—
Yes, wherever the Wine-god has turned his handsome head.
So let us duly pay to that god the homage we owe him
In anthems our fathers sang, in offerings of fruit and cake:
Led by the horn, let the ritual goat be stood at the altar,   395
And the rich meat of the sacrifice roast upon hazel spits.
    Another task there is, the dressing of vines, that is never
Finished: for year by year
Three times, four times you should loosen the soil: you can-
      not turn
And break the clods with your hoe too often; the whole
      plantation's   400

fronde nemus. redit agricolis labor actus in orbem,
atque in se sua per vestigia volvitur annus.
ac iam olim, seras posuit cum vinea frondes
frigidus et silvis Aquilo decussit honorem,
iam tum acer curas venientem extendit in annum   405
rusticus, et curvo Saturni dente relictam
persequitur vitem attondens fingitque putando.
primus humum fodito, primus devecta cremato
sarmenta, et vallos primus sub tecta referto;
postremus metito. bis vitibus ingruit umbra,   410
bis segetem densis obducunt sentibus herbae;
durus uterque labor: laudato ingentia rura,
exiguum colito. nec non etiam aspera rusci
vimina per silvam et ripis fluvialis harundo
caeditur, incultique exercet cura salicti.   415
iam vinctae vites, iam falcem arbusta reponunt,
iam canit effectos extremus vinitor antes:
sollicitanda tamen tellus pulvisque movendus,
et iam maturis metuendus Iuppiter uvis.
   Contra non ulla est oleis cultura: neque illae   420
procurvam exspectant falcem rastrosque tenacis,
cum semel haeserunt arvis aurasque tulerunt;
ipsa satis tellus, cum dente recluditur unco,
sufficit umorem et gravidas cum vomere fruges.
hoc pinguem et placitam Paci nutritor olivam.   425
   Poma quoque, ut primum truncos sensere valentis

Load of shade must be lightened. A farmer's work proceeds in
Cycles, as the shuttling year returns on its own track.
And now, the time when a vineyard puts off its reluctant
    leaves
And a bitter north wind has blown away the pride of the
    woodland,
Even now the countryman actively pushes on to the com-
    ing   405
Year and its tasks; attacking the naked vine with a curved
Pruning-knife, he shears and trims it into shape.
Be the first to dig the land, the first to wheel off the prunings
For the bonfire, the first to bring your vine-poles under
    cover;
But the last to gather the vintage. Twice will the vines grow
    thick   410
With shade, and twice will a tangle of briars overrun the
    vineyards;
Each makes for hard work: so admire a large estate if you
    like,
But farm a small one. Further,
You'll find rough broom in the woods and reeds on the river
    bank
To be cut, and the willow beds will give you plenty of
    work.   415
Now the vines are tied, the plants are done with pruning,
The last vine-dresser sings over his finished labours,
Yet still you must keep the soil busy, the dust on the move,
And watch apprehensive for weather which threatens the
    ripening grape
  Olives are just the opposite: they require no cultiva-
    tion   420
And have no use for the sickle knife or the stiff-tooth rake
Once they've dug themselves in on the fields and stood up
    to winds.
Earth herself, by the crooked plough laid bare, provides
Moisture enough for the plants and a heavy crop from the
    ploughshare.
Thus shall you breed the rich olive, beloved of Peace.   425
  Orchards too, when once they have tasted the power in
    their trunks

et viris habuere suas, ad sidera raptim
vi propria nituntur opisque haud indiga nostrae.
nec minus interea fetu nemus omne gravescit,
sanguineisque inculta rubent aviaria bacis.　　　　　430
tondentur cytisi, taedas silva alta ministrat,
pascunturque ignes nocturni et lumina fundunt.
et dubitant homines serere atque impendere curam?
　　quid maiora sequar? salices humilesque genistae
aut illae pecori frondem aut pastoribus umbram　　435
sufficiunt saepemque satis et pabula melli.
et iuvat undantem buxo spectare Cytorum
Naryciaeque picis lucos, iuvat arva videre
non rastris, hominum non ulli obnoxia curae.
　　ipsae Caucasio steriles in vertice silvae,　　　　440
quas animosi Euri adsidue franguntque feruntque,
dant alios aliae fetus, dant utile lignum
navigiis pinus, domibus cedrumque cupressosque.
hinc radios trivere rotis, hinc tympana plaustris
agricolae, et pandas ratibus posuere carinas.　　　445
viminibus salices, fecundae frondibus ulmi,
at myrtus validis hastilibus et bona bello
cornus, Ituraeos taxi torquentur in arcus.
nec tiliae leves aut torno rasile buxum
non formam accipiunt ferroque cavantur acuto.　　450
nec non et torrentem undam levis innatat alnus
missa Pado; nec non et apes examina condunt
corticibusque cavis vitiosaeque ilicis alvo.
quid memorandum aeque Baccheia dona tulerunt?
Bacchus et ad culpam causas dedit; ille furentis　　455
Centauros leto domuit, Rhoetumque Pholumque

And realized their own strength, race up to the stars by nature
Needing no help from us.
No less does the wildwood also come out with fruits galore,
And blood-red berries like rubies adorn the untilled bird-
    land.   430
There's clover to be cut, firewood gleaned in the forest:
Night-long the fires are fed, and their light is pooled around.
Do men still hesitate to sow and take some trouble?

    Why should I stick to big trees? Willow and humble broom
Give plenty of leaf to cattle and shade enough for a
    shepherd,   435
Hedges they make for crops and a feed for the honey-bee.
Pleasant it is to behold the box trees wave on Cytorus,
Groves of Narycian pine, fields under no obligation
To man or his implements.

    Even the fruitless forests you find on peaks of
    Caucasus,   440
For ever torn and tossed by the storm-breathing east wind,
Yield each a special product—pine wood that's used in ship-
    yards,
Cedar and cypress wood that go to the building of houses.
From wood the countryman turns the spokes for wheels and
    the waggon's
Solid wheels, and wooden the keels you lay down for
    ships.   445
Willows provide our withies, elms leaf-fodder for cattle,
But myrtle bears tough spear-shafts, cornel your cavalry-
    lances
Good in battle, while bows from Iturean yew are fashioned.
Smooth lime and box which the lathe
Has shaved take shape as well, are chamfered with sharp
    chisels.   450
The alder too, when you launch it upon the Po, rides lightly
That boiling stream; while bees are used to hide their swarms
Within some hollow bark or the heart of a rotten ilex.
What has the Wine-god given so thoroughly worth our
    thanks?
Much, indeed, he has done deserving blame. It was he   455
Who maddened and killed the Centaurs, and Rhoetus and
    Pholus, and made

et magno Hylaeum Lapithis cratere minantem.

O fortunatos nimium, sua si bona norint,
agricolas, quibus ipsa procul discordibus armis
fundit humo facilem victum iustissima tellus! 460
si non ingentem foribus domus alta superbis
mane salutantum totis vomit aedibus undam,
nec varios inhiant pulchra testudine postis,
inlusasque auro vestis Ephyreiaque aera,
alba neque Assyrio fucatur lana veneno, 465
nec casia liquidi corrumpitur usus olivi;
at secura quies et nescia fallere vita,
dives opum variarum, at latis otia fundis,
speluncae, vivique lacus, et frigida Tempe,
mugitusque boum, mollesque sub arbore somni 470
non absunt; illic saltus ac lustra ferarum,
et patiens operum exiguoque adsueta iuventus,
sacra deum, sanctique patres; extrema per illos
Iustitia excedens terris vestigia fecit.

Me vero primum dulces ante omnia Musae, 475
quarum sacra fero ingenti percussus amore,
accipiant, caelique vias et sidera monstrent,
defectus solis varios lunaeque labores;
unde tremor terris, qua vi maria alta tumescant
obicibus ruptis rursusque in se ipsa residant, 480
quid tantum Oceano properent se tingere soles
hiberni, vel quae tardis mora noctibus obstet.
sin has ne possim naturae accedere partis
frigidus obstiterit circum praecordia sanguis,
rura mihi et rigui placeant in vallibus amnes, 485
flumina amem silvasque inglorius. o ubi campi
Spercheusque et virginibus bacchata Lacaenis
Taygeta! o qui me gelidis invallibus Haemi
sistat, et ingenti ramorum protegat umbra!

Hylaeus brawl and go for the Lapithae with a bottle.

   Oh, too lucky for words, if only he knew his luck,
Is the countryman who far from the clash of armaments
Lives, and rewarding earth is lavish of all he needs!   460
True, no mansion tall with a swanky gate throws up
In the morning a mob of callers to crowd him out and gape at
Doorposts inlaid with beautiful tortoiseshell, attire
Of gold brocade, connoisseur's bronzes.

No foreign dyes may stain his white fleeces, nor exotic   465
Spice like cinnamon spoil his olive oil for use:
But calm security and a life that will not cheat you,
Rich in its own rewards, are here: the broad ease of the
   farmlands,
Caves, living lakes, and combes that are cool even at mid-
   summer
Mooing of herds, and slumber mild in the trees' shade.   470
Here are glades game-haunted,
Lads hardened to labour, inured to simple ways,
Reverence for God, respect for the family. When Justice
Left earth, her latest footprints were stamped on folk like
   these.

   Since Poetry for me comes first—my goddess and chief
   delight   475
Whose devotee I am, with a master-passion adoring—
I wish above all she accept me, revealing the stars and the
   sky-routes,
The several eclipses of the sun, the moon pallid in labour,
The cause of earthquakes and the force that compels the
   deepsea
To swell, to break all bounds, to fall back on itself again;   480
The reason why winter suns race on to dip in the ocean,
And what delays the long nights.
But if a sluggishness, a lack of heat in my heart's blood
Denies me access to these mysteries of the universe,
Then let the country charm me, the rivers that channel its
   valleys,   485
Then may I love its forest and stream, and let fame go hang.
Oh for the plain of Spercheus, Taÿgeta where the Spartan
Girls run mad! And oh for one to stay me in Haemus'
Cool glens, and comfort me in a world of branchy shade!

felix qui potuit rerum cognoscere causas,   490
atque metus omnis et inexorabile fatum
subiecit pedibus strepitumque Acherontis avari.
fortunatus et ille deos qui novit agrestis—
Panaque Silvanumque senem Nymphasque sorores.
illum non populi fasces, non purpura regum   495
flexit et infidos agitans discordia fratres,
aut coniurato descendens Dacus ab Histro,
non res Romanae perituraque regna: neque ille
aut doluit miserans inopem aut invidit habenti.
quos rami fructus, quos ipsa volentia rura   500
sponte tulere sua, carpsit, nec ferrea iura
insanumque forum aut populi tabularia vidit.
sollicitant alii remis freta caeca, ruuntque
in ferrum, penetrant aulas et limina regum;
hic petit excidiis urbem miserosque Penatis,   505
ut gemma bibat et Sarrano dormiat ostro;
condit opes alius defossoque incubat auro;
hic stupet attonitus rostris; hunc plausus hiantem
per cuneos geminatus enim plebisque patrumque
corripuit; gaudent perfusi sanguine fratrum,   510
exsilioque domos et dulcia limina mutant
atque alio patriam quaerunt sub sole iacentem.
  agricola incurvo terram dimovit aratro:
hinc anni labor, hinc patriam parvosque nepotes
sustinet, hinc armenta boum meritosque iuvencos.   515
nec requies, quin aut pomis exuberet annus
aut fetu pecorum aut Cerealis mergite culmi,
proventuque oneret sulcos atque horrea vincat.
venit hiems: teritur Sicyonia baca trapetis,
glande sues laeti redeunt, dant arbuta silvae;   520

Lucky is he who can learn the roots of the universe,   490
Has mastered all his fears and fate's intransigence
And the hungry clamour of hell.
But fortunate too the man who is friends with the country
    gods—
Pan and old Silvanus and the sisterhood of nymphs:
The fasces have no power to disturb him, nor the purple   495
Of monarchs, nor civil war that sets brother at brother's throat,
Nor yet the scheming Dacian as he marches down from the
    Danube,
Nor the Roman Empire itself and kingdoms falling to ruin.
He has no poor to pity, no envy for the rich.
The fruit on the bough, the crops that the field is glad to
    bear   500
Are his for the gathering: he spares not a glance for the iron
Rigour of law, the municipal racket, the public records.
Other men dare the sea with their oars blindly, or dash
On the sword, or insinuate themselves into royal courts:
One ruins a whole town and the tenements of the poor   505
In his lust for jewelled cups, for scarlet linen to sleep on;
One piles up great wealth, gloats over his cache of gold;
One gawps at the public speakers; one is worked up to
    hysteria
By the plaudits of senate and people resounding across the
    benches:
These shed their brothers' blood   510
Merrily, they barter for exile their homes beloved
And leave for countries lying under an alien sun.
    But still the farmer furrows the land with his curving
    plough:
The land is his annual labour, it keeps his native country,
His little grandsons and herds of cattle and trusty bull-
    ocks.   515
Unresting the year teems with orchard fruit, or young
Of cattle, or sheaves of corn,
Brimming the furrows with plenty, overflowing the barns.
Winter comes, when olives are crushed in the press, and pigs
Return elate with acorns, and woods give arbutus
    berries: 520

et varios ponit fetus autumnus, et alte
mitis in apricis coquitur vindemia saxis.
interea dulces pendent circum oscula nati,
casta pudicitiam servat domus, ubera vaccae
lactea demittunt, pinguesque in gramine laeto   525
inter se adversis luctantur cornibus haedi.
ipse dies agitat festos fususque per herbam,
ignis ubi in medio et socii cratera coronant,
te libans, Lenaee, vocat pecorisque magistris
velocis iaculi certamina ponit in ulmo,   530
corporaque agresti nudant praedura palaestrae.
hanc olim veteres vitam coluere Sabini,
hanc Remus et frater, sic fortis Etruria crevit
scilicet et rerum facta est pulcherrima Roma,
septemque una sibi muro circumdedit arces.   535
ante etiam sceptrum Dictaei regis et ante
impia quam caesis gens est epulata iuvencis,
aureus hanc vitam in terris Saturnus agebat;
necdum etiam audierant inflari classica, necdum
impositos duris crepitare incudibus ensis.   540
    Sed nos immensum spatiis confecimus aequor,
et iam tempus equum fumantia solvere colla.

Autumn drops her varied fruits at our feet, while far
Above on sunny rocks the vintage basks and mellows.
And all the time he has dear children who dote on kisses,
A house that preserves the tradition of chastity, cows that
    hang
Their milky udders, and plump young goats on the happy
    green   525
Romping and butting with their horns.
The farmer himself keeps holidays when, at ease in a meadow,
A fire in the midst and friends there to crown the flowing
    bowl,
He drinks the health of the Wine-god and arranges for his
    herdsmen
A darts-match, setting up the target upon an elm tree,   530
And the labourers bare their sinewy bodies for country
    wrestling.
Such was the life the Sabines lived in days of old,
And Remus and his brother: so it was beyond all question
That Tuscany grew to greatness, Rome became queen of the
    world
Ringing her seven citadels with a single wall.   535
Before the rise of the Cretan
Lord, before impious men slaughtered bullocks for the
    banquet,
Such was the life that golden Saturn lived upon earth:
Mankind had not yet heard the bugle bellow for war,
Not yet heard the clank of the sword on the hard
    anvil. . . .   540
  But we have covered a deal of ground in our course, and
    now
It's time to slip off the harness from the necks of our reeking
    horses.

LIBER III

Te quoque, magna Pales, et te memorande canemus
pastor ab Amphryso, vos, silvae amnesque Lycaei.
cetera, quae vacuas tenuissent carmina mentes,
omnia iam vulgata: quis aut Eurysthea durum,
aut inlaudati nescit Busiridis aras?   5
cui non dictus Hylas puer, et Latonia Delos,
Hippodameque, umeroque Pelops insignis eburno,
acer equis? temptanda via est, qua me quoque possim
tollere humo victorque virum volitare per ora.
primus ego in patriam mecum, modo vita supersit,   10
Aonio rediens deducam vertice Musas;
primus Idumaeas referam tibi, Mantua, palmas;
et viridi in campo templum de marmore ponam
propter aquam, tardis ingens ubi flexibus errat
Mincius et tenera praetexit harundine ripas.   15
in medio mihi Caesar erit templumque tenebit:
illi victor ego et Tyrio conspectus in ostro
centum quadriiugos agitabo ad flumina currus.
cuncta mihi Alpheum linquens lucosque Molorchi
cursibus et crudo decernet Graecia caestu.   20
ipse caput tonsae foliis ornatus olivae
dona feram. iam nunc sollemnis ducere pompas
ad delubra iuvat caesosque videre iuvencos,
vel scaena ut versis discedat frontibus utque
purpurea intexti tollant aulaea Britanni.   25

BOOK 3

You too, great goddess of sheepfolds, I'm going to sing, and
    you
Apollo, a shepherd once, and the woods and streams of
    Arcadia.
Other themes, which might have pleasured an idle mind,
Are hackneyed all of them: everyone's heard of cruel
Eurystheus and the outrageous altar Busiris built.   5
Who does not know about Hylas, Latona who lived on Delos,
Hippodame and Pelops that horseman heroic, renowned
For his ivory shoulder? No, I must venture a theme will
    exalt me
From earth and give me wings and a triumph on every
    tongue.
If life enough is left me,   10
I'll be the first to bring the Muse of song to my birthplace
From Greece, and wear the poet's palm for Mantua;
And there in the green meadows I'll build a shrine of marble
Close to the waterside, where the river Mincius wanders
With lazy loops and fringes the banks with delicate reed.   15
Caesar's image shall stand there in the midst, commanding
    my temple,
While I, like a victor, conspicuous in crimson robes, shall drive
A hundred four-horse chariots up and down by the river.
All Greece will leave Alpheus and the Peloponnesian groves
To take part in the races and boxing-bouts I've arranged.   20
I myself, wearing a chaplet of trimmed olive,
Will present the prizes. How nice now
To lead the ritual walk to the shrine and watch the sacrifice,
Or to stare at the stage revealed when the scenes are shifted
And the crimson curtain rising embroidered with figures of
    Britons.   25

in foribus pugnam ex auro solidoque elephanto
Gangaridum faciam victorisque arma Quirini,
atque hic undantem bello magnumque fluentem
Nilum, ac navali surgentis aere columnas.
addam urbes Asiae domitas pulsumque Niphaten   30
fidentemque fuga Parthum versisque sagittis;
et duo rapta manu diverso ex hoste tropaea
bisque triumphatas utroque ab litore gentis.
stabunt et Parii lapides, spirantia signa,
Assaraci proles demissaeque ab Iove gentis   35
nomina, Trosque parens et Troiae Cynthius auctor.
Invidia infelix Furias amnemque severum
Cocyti metuet tortosque Ixionis anguis
immanemque rotam et non exsuperabile saxum.
interea Dryadum silvas saltusque sequamur   40
intactos, tua, Maecenas, haud mollia iussa.
te sine nil altum mens incohat. en age segnis
rumpe moras; vocat ingenti clamore Cithaeron
Taygetique canes domitrixque Epidaurus equorum,
et vox adsensu nemorum ingeminata remugit.   45
mox tamen ardentis accingar dicere pugnas
Caesaris, et nomen fama tot ferre per annos
Tithoni prima quot abest ab origine Caesar.

  Seu quis Olympiacae miratus praemia palmae
pascit equos, seu quis fortis ad aratra iuvencos,   50
corpora praecipue matrum legat. optima torvae
forma bovis cui turpe caput, cui plurima cervix,
et crurum tenus a mento palearia pendent;
tum longo nullus lateri modus; omnia magna,
pes etiam; et camuris hirtae sub cornibus aures.   55
nec mihi displiceat maculis insignis et albo,
aut iuga detrectans interdumque aspera cornu
et faciem tauro propior, quaeque ardua tota,

On the doors of my temple I'll have engraved in gold and solid
Ivory a battle scene—the Romans beating the Indians,
And here the enormous stream of Nile a-surge with a naval
Battle, and columns rising cast from the bronze of warships.
I'll add the cities of Asia we've mastered, Armenians
routed,   30
Parthians whose forte is flight and shooting over their
shoulder;
Two trophies taken in battle from different foes, a double
Triumph from either shore.
Parian stone shall stand there, breathing monuments—
The brood of Assaracus, our genealogy from Jove,   35
Tros our ancestor, and Apollo founder of Troy.
Envious men shall gaze in fear at the Furies, the pitiless
River of Hell, Ixion lashed with writhing snakes
To his giant wheel, and the rock that Sisyphus can't stop
rolling.
Meanwhile let us pursue the woodland ways, the virgin   40
Lawns, my friend, the difficult task you have laid upon me.
Without your help, my spirit lacks high ambition. Come then,
Break up my lassitude! Loud is Cithaeron calling
And the hounds of Taÿgetus and Epidaurus tamer of horses,
And the woods all answer Yes and echo the call again.   45
Yet soon will I stir myself
To tell of Caesar's furious battles, to give him fame
For as many years as divide his day from the birth of
Tithonus.

Suppose you covet the prize at Olympia and breed horses,
Or suppose you're breeding bullocks strong-bodied for the
plough,   50
The chief thing is the choosing of dams. In a cow the following
Points should be looked for—a rough appearance, a coarse
head,
Generous neck, and dewlaps hanging from jaw to leg;
Flanks as roomy as you like; everything built on a large scale,
Even the hoof; and shaggy ears under the crooked horns.   55
I have nothing against an animal of prominent white markings,
Or one that rejects the yoke and is hasty at times with her
horn—
More like a bull to look at,

et gradiens ima verrit vestigia cauda.
aetas Lucinam iustosque pati hymenaeos   60
desinit ante decem, post quattuor incipit annos;
cetera nec feturae habilis nec fortis aratris.
interea, superat gregibus dum laeta iuventas,
solve mares; mitte in Venerem pecuaria primus,
atque aliam ex alia generando suffice prolem.   65
optima quaeque dies miseris mortalibus aevi
prima fugit: subeunt morbi tristisque senectus
et labor, et durae rapit inclementia mortis.
semper erunt quarum mutari corpora malis:
semper enim refice ac, ne post amissa requiras,   70
ante veni, et subolem armento sortire quotannis.
    Nec non et pecori est idem dilectus equino.
tu modo, quos in spem statues summittere gentis,
praecipuum iam inde a teneris impende laborem.
continuo pecoris generosi pullus in arvis   75
altius ingreditur et mollia crura reponit;
primus et ire viam et fluvios temptare minantis
audet, et ignoto sese committere ponti,
nec vanos horret strepitus. illi ardua cervix
argutumque caput, brevis alvus obesaque terga,   80
luxuriatque toris animosum pectus: (honesti
spadices glaucique, color deterrimus albis
et gilvo). tum, si qua sonum procul arma dedere,
stare loco nescit, micat auribus et tremit artus,
collectumque fremens volvit sub naribus ignem.   85
densa iuba, et dextro iactata recumbit in armo;
at duplex agitur per lumbos spina, cavatque
tellurem et solido graviter sonat ungula cornu.
talis Amyclaei domitus Pollucis habenis

Tall all over, dusting the ground with her tail as she goes.
The proper period for a cow to mate and calve   60
Ends before the tenth, begins after the fourth year:
For the rest she is neither fit for breeding nor strong for
    ploughing.
Within these limits, while the herd is young and lusty,
Loose the males, early give over your cattle to love,
Keep up your stock by breeding from one to the next
    generation.   65
Of the measure of days allowed to piteous mortals, the best
    days
Are first to leave: illness and sorry old age loom up,
Suffering and death's untender mercies take all away.
Some beasts there will always be
That you wish to exchange: replace them, of course; and to
    compensate   70
For their loss, be quick to choose the young of the herd each
    year.
  Equal care must be exercised in the picking of horseflesh.
It's essential that those you wish to rear for stud should receive
Particular attention right from the very start.
Notice a thoroughbred foal in the paddock—how from
    birth   75
He picks his feet up high, stepping fastidiously;
First of the herd he'll venture onto the highroad, and ford
The menacing river, and brave the unknown dangers of
    bridges;
Nor will he shy at a meaningless noise. He shows a proud
    neck,
A finely tapering head, short barrel and fleshy back,   80
And his spirited chest ripples with muscle: (bays and roans
Are soundest, white or dun
Horses the worst). If he hears armour clang in the distance,
He can't keep still, the ears prick up, the limbs quiver,
He drinks the air, he jets it in hot steam out of his nostrils.   85
The mane is thick, and tumbles on the right shoulder when
    tossed:
The spine runs over the loins, sunk between two ridges;
The solid hoof makes a deep clatter and hurls up divots.
Such a horse was Cyllarus, that Pollux broke in; and such were

Cyllarus et, quorum Grai meminere poetae,   90
Martis equi biiuges et magni currus Achilli.
talis et ipse iubam cervice effundit equina
coniugis adventu pernix Saturnus, et altum
Pelion hinnitu fugiens implevit acuto.

   Hunc quoque, ubi aut morbo gravis aut iam segnior annis
deficit, abde domo nec turpi ignosce senectae.   96
frigidus in Venerem senior, frustraque laborem
ingratum trahit, et, si quando ad proelia ventum est,
ut quondam in stipulis magnus sine viribus ignis,
incassum furit. ergo animos aevumque notabis   100
praecipue: hinc alias artis prolemque parentum
et quis cuique dolor victo, quae gloria palmae.
nonne vides, cum praecipiti certamine campum
corripuere, ruuntque effusi carcere currus,
cum spes adrectae iuvenum, exsultantiaque haurit   105
corda pavor pulsans? illi instant verbere torto
et proni dant lora, volat vi fervidus axis;
iamque humiles, iamque elati sublime videntur
aëra per vacuum ferri atque adsurgere in auras;
nec mora nec requies; at fulvae nimbus harenae   110
tollitur, umescunt spumis flatuque sequentum:
tantus amor laudum, tantae est victoria curae.
primus Erichthonius currus et quattuor ausus
iungere equos, rapidusque rotis insistere victor.
frena Pelethronii Lapithae gyrosque dedere   115
impositi dorso: atque equitem docuere sub armis
insultare solo et gressus glomerare superbos.
aequus uterque labor, aeque iuvenemque magistri

The two-yoke team of the War-god   90
And the horses of great Achilles, mentioned by Greek poets.
Such the guise that Saturn assumed to escape his wife,
A horse-mane streaming over his neck as he streaked away
And made the peaks of Pelion resound with a stallion's
     neighing.
     Yet even that horse, when he weakens from illness or
          weight of years,   95
You must pension off and spare no pity for age's failings.
To be old is to be cold in rut, to prolong a loveless
Labour impotently; and whenever it comes to the conflict,
The flame is no more than a crackling of thorns, a foolish fury.
So mark them for youth and mettle   100
Above all: and next for other merits—their parents' pedigree,
The prizes and beatings they've taken, and how they've
     taken each.
Now look! It's a chariot race! They've charged from the
     starting-gate,
They're galloping down the course all out, they're covering
     the ground!
Each driver's hope runs high; his heart is drained with
     terror,   105
Drumming with mad excitement: the drivers whirling their
     whips,
Leaning forward, giving the horses their head, the hot wheels
     flying,
Now *ventre-à-terre* they seem to travel, and then bouncing
High to be twitched through the air and trying to soar on
     the breezes;
No slackening or respite: the course is a cloud of yellow
     dust,   110
The drivers are wet with the spindrift breath of the horses
     behind them.
So keen they are for the laurels, and victory means so much.
Erichthon thought of the four-horse
Chariot first, and rode a winning race on its wheels.
The Lapithae, celebrated horsemen, invented the bridle   115
And the training-ring: it was they who taught cavalrymen
The arts of the *haute école*.
Racers and chargers are both a job to breed: for either

exquirunt calidumque animis et cursibus acrem—
quamvis saepe fuga versos ille egerit hostis,   120
et patriam Epirum referat fortisque Mycenas
Neptunique ipsa deducat origine gentem.

His animadversis instant sub tempus et omnis
impendunt curas denso distendere pingui
quem legere ducem et pecori dixere maritum: 125
florentisque secant herbas fluviosque ministrant
farraque, ne blando nequeat superesse labori
invalidique patrum referant ieiunia nati.
ipsa autem macie tenuant armenta volentes,
atque, ubi concubitus primos iam nota voluptas   130
sollicitat, frondesque negant et fontibus arcent.
saepe etiam cursu quatiunt et sole fatigant,
cum graviter tunsis gemit area frugibus, et cum
surgentem ad Zephyrum paleae iactantur inanes.
hoc faciunt, nimio ne luxu obtunsior usus   135
sit genitali arvo et sulcos oblimet inertis,
sed rapiat sitiens Venerem interiusque recondat.

Rursus cura patrum cadere et succedere matrum
incipit. exactis gravidae cum mensibus errant:
non illas gravibus quisquam iuga ducere plaustris,   140
non saltu superare viam sit passus et acri
carpere prata fuga fluviosque innare rapacis.
saltibus in vacuis pascunt et plena secundum
flumina, muscus ubi et viridissima gramine ripa,
speluncaeque tegant et saxea procubet umbra.   145
est lucos Silari circa ilicibusque virentem

It's youth, mettle and pace that trainers first demand—
No matter how often a horse may have charged and routed
    the foe,   120
No matter if he come from Epirus or brave Mycenae
Or trace his pedigree back even to Neptune's stable.

    Bearing in mind all this, they are forewarned and busy
To feed high and fill out with solid flesh the stallion
Whom they have chosen leader and bridegroom-lord of the
    herd: 125
They cut the flowering clover, they provide water and corn,
Lest the pleasured work be too much for him, and weakly sons
Prove the sire undernourished.
But the dams they deliberately keep hungry to fine them
    down;
And when the instinctive lust for mating first shall tease
    them,   130
They let them have no leaves and fence them away from
    water:
Often too they make them gallop and sweat in the sun
When threshing-floors groan heavily under the pounding
    flail
And empty chaff is wafted about on a freshening west wind.
This they do lest the breeding ground be dulled by indul-
    gence,   135
The furrows clogged and inert
That should fasten thirstily on love and bury it far within.

    The care of the sires becomes less important now, and the
    dams
Need more attention. Their months are run, they are long in
    foal now:
Madness to yoke them and make them haul your heavy
    waggons,   140
To let them clear the road at a leap or gallop over
Meadows in breakneck flight or swim the racing rivers:
But rather let them feed in roomy meads, along
Full streams, where moss is growing and the bank most
    green with grass,
And caves give shelter and cliffs lean out in lengthening
    shadow.   145
About the groves of Silarus and Alburnus evergreen

plurimus Alburnum volitans, cui nomen asilo
Romanum est, oestrum Grai vertere vocantes,
asper, acerba sonans, quo tota exterrita silvis
diffugiunt armenta, furit mugitibus aether   150
concussus silvaeque et sicci ripa Tanagri.
hoc quondam monstro horribilis exercuit iras
Inachiae Iuno pestem meditata iuvencae.
hunc quoque, nam mediis fervoribus acrior instat,
arcebis gravido pecori, armentaque pasces   155
sole recens orto aut noctem ducentibus astris.
  Post partum cura in vitulos traducitur omnis:
continuoque notas et nomina gentis inurunt,
et quos aut pecori malint summittere habendo
aut aris servare sacros aut scindere terram   160
et campum horrentem fractis invertere glaebis.
cetera pascuntur viridis armenta per herbas:
tu quos ad studium atque usum formabis agrestem
iam vitulos hortare viamque insiste domandi,
dum faciles animi iuvenum, dum mobilis aetas.   165
ac primum laxos tenui de vimine circlos
cervici subnecte; dehinc, ubi libera colla
servitio adsuerint, ipsis e torquibus aptos
iunge pares, et coge gradum conferre iuvencos;
atque illis iam saepe rotae ducantur inanes   170
per terram, et summo vestigia pulvere signent:
post valido nitens sub pondere faginus axis
instrepat, et iunctos temo trahat aereus orbis.
interea pubi indomitae non gramina tantum
nec vescas salicum frondes ulvamque palustrem,   175
sed frumenta manu carpes sata; nec tibi fetae

In holm-oak swarms an insect
We call the gadfly ('oestrus' is the Greek name for it)—
A brute with a shrill buzz that drives whole herds crazy
Scattering through the woods, till sky and woods and the
    banks of   150
Bone-dry rivers are stunned and go mad with their bellowing.
Juno once, giving rein to horrible rage, decided
To plague with this pest the heifer-daughter of Inachus.
This fly, which is most ferocious in the heat of summer noons,
You must keep from your breeding cattle and bring the herd
    to pasture   155
When the sun's but newly risen or the stars are fetching the
    night.

   After birth, your care is all transferred to the calves:
At once you will brand the mark of their breed on those you
    wish
To rear for raising stock,
For sacrifice at the altar, or for tilling the soil   160
And turning the broken clods across the puckered plain.
The rest of the herd are put out to graze on the meadow
    grasses:
But those you would train for the practice and profit of
    agriculture
At a tender age you'll take in hand and set on the right road
Of discipline, while their mind is unformed, their youth
    docile.   165
First, tie around the neck a loose halter of light withy:
Next, when the neck that was free
Has bowed to bondage, use these same halters for yoking
Matched pairs of bullocks together, and make them walk in
    step:
Let them draw empty carts now, time and time again   170
Over the ground, and groove a light track in the dust:
After this may the beechen axles strain with a big load
Creaking, the linked wheels be drawn by the copper-edged
    shaft.
While they are yet unbroken, you'll cut for them not only
Hay and the fine leaves of the willow and fenny sedge,   175
But corn in the blade. Don't follow our forbears' custom,
    whereby

more patrum nivea implebunt mulctraria vaccae,
sed tota in dulcis consument ubera natos.
   Sin ad bella magis studium turmasque ferocis,
aut Alphea rotis praelabi flumina Pisae   180
et Iovis in luco currus agitare volantis,
primus equi labor est animos atque arma videre
bellantum lituosque pati, tractuque gementem
ferre rotam et stabulo frenos audire sonantis;
tum magis atque magis blandis gaudere magistri   185
laudibus et plausae sonitum cervicis amare.
atque haec iam primo depulsus ab ubere matris
audeat, inque vicem det mollibus ora capistris
invalidus etiamque tremens, etiam inscius aevi.
at tribus exactis ubi quarta accesserit aestas,   190
carpere mox gyrum incipiat gradibusque sonare
compositis sinuetque alterna volumina crurum,
sitque laboranti similis; tum cursibus auras
tum vocet, ac per aperta volans ceu liber habenis
aequora vix summa vestigia ponat harena,   195
qualis Hyperboreis Aquilo cum densus ab oris
incubuit, Scythiaeque hiemes atque arida differt
nubila: tum segetes altae campique natantes
lenibus horrescunt flabris, summaeque sonorem
dant silvae, longique urgent ad litora fluctus;   200
ille volat simul arva fuga, simul aequora verrens.
hic vel ad Elei metas et maxima campi
sudabit spatia et spumas aget ore cruentas,
bellica vel molli melius feret esseda collo.
tum demum crassa magnum farragine corpus   205
crescere iam domitis sinito: namque ante domandum
ingentis tollent animos, prensique negabunt

Mother-cows filled the snowy milk-pails: their young should
    have all
The benefit of their udders.

  But if your aim is rather to breed cavalry horses,
Or go in for chariot-racing at the Olympic games   180
Hurtling along by Alpheus in the grove of Jupiter's house,
First you will train the horse to watch the pride and panoply
Of regiments, to stand the bugle, or bear the squeal of
Dragging wheels and hear the jangle of harness in stable:
Then, little by little, the trainer wheedles him   185
To love a word of praise and the sound of his neck being
    patted.
This he may do when barely weaned, and try a rope-bit
In his mouth now and then
Though weak and wambling still, unaware of his growing
    power.
But when he's a three-year-old and his fourth summer is
    here,   190
Let him start presently to pace the ring and step
Harmoniously and learn to move at a limber stride
And begin to look like a worker. Then will he challenge the
    wind
To a race, and as if he were free of the rein fly over the open
Downs and leave but the lightest print of his hoof on the
    dust,   195
Like a north wind when from the frontiers of ice in gathering
    force
It swoops, drives helter-skelter the cold dry northern clouds:
The cornfields deep and the deepsea
Shudder with the gusts that flick them, and treetops in the
    forest
Cry aloud, and long rollers ride to the beach: 200
So flies that wind, sweeping field and flood as it goes.
Either that horse, sweating, mouth flecked with bloody foam,
Will last the distance at Elis and pass the finishing-post,
Or his pliant neck is better in harness pulling a curricle.
Then at last, when they're broken in, fill out their bodies 205
With coarse mixed mash: for until
You break them, their hearts are too high-flown, they jib at
    handling,

verbera lenta pati et duris parere lupatis.
    Sed non ulla magis viris industria firmat
quam Venerem et caeci stimulos avertere amoris,   210
sive boum sive est cui gratior usus equorum.
atque ideo tauros procul atque in sola relegant
pascua post montem oppositum et trans flumina lata,
aut intus clausos satura ad praesepia servant.
carpit enim viris paulatim uritque videndo   215
femina, nec nemorum patitur meminisse nec herbae
dulcibus illa quidem inlecebris, et saepe superbos
cornibus inter se subigit decernere amantis.
pascitur in magna Sila formosa iuvenca:
illi alternantes multa vi proelia miscent   220
vulneribus crebris, lavit ater corpora sanguis,
versaque in obnixos urgentur cornua vasto
cum gemitu, reboant silvaeque et longus Olympus.
nec mos bellantis una stabulare, sed alter
victus abit longeque ignotis exsulat oris,   225
multa gemens ignominiam plagasque superbi
victoris, tum quos amisit inultus amores;
et stabula aspectans regnis excessit avitis.
ergo omni cura viris exercet et inter
dura iacet pernix instrato saxa cubili,   230
frondibus hirsutis et carice pastus acuta,
et temptat sese atque irasci in cornua discit
arboris obnixus trunco, ventosque lacessit
ictibus, et sparsa ad pugnam proludit harena.
post ubi collectum robur viresque refectae,   235
signa movet praecepsque oblitum fertur in hostem:
fluctus uti medio coepit cum albescere ponto,
longius ex altoque sinum trahit, utque volutus
ad terras immane sonat per saxa neque ipso
monte minor procumbit, at ima exaestuat unda   240

Refuse to bear the lash or obey the cruel curb.

But the most effective way to reinforce their strength

Is to bar them off from the passion and blinding goads of
lust,   210

Whether your fancy is the breeding of bulls or horses.

Therefore they relegate the bull to a lonely pasture

Far away, railed off by a mountain and broad rivers,

Or to solitary confinement within the farm's rich stall.

For the female fritters away his strength and burns him
up   215

With gazing at her, and makes him forget the woods and
meadows—

So sweet her enticement—and often

Compels her proud lovers to fight it out with their horns.

A handsome heifer is grazing upon the slopes of Sila:

Two bulls begin to encounter furiously and inflict   220

Many gashes, until their bodies are dark with blood;

Their horns confront, lock with a crash and take the strain,

The forests and far-reaching skies roar back at them.

Nor is it the way of the fighters to herd together; the one

Defeated goes into retirement far off in unknown
regions,   225

Groaning much at his own humiliation, the blows of

The cocky victor, the loss of a love not yet avenged;

He looks around his stall, then leaves that ancestral kingdom.

Therefore he trains assiduously, and lies untiring

On a makeshift bed among   230

Flint rocks, and feeds upon rough leaves and pointed reed-
grass:

He practises putting all his fury into his horns

By goring trunks of trees, he butts at the air in anger,

He paws and tosses the sand as a prelude of coming battle.

Afterwards, his strength collected, his powers repaired, 235

He advances and hurtles headlong on the foe who has forgot
him:

As when a wave begins to whiten out in mid-ocean

It draws a swelling curve far off from the deep, and landwards

Rolling roars tremendous among the rocks and falls

Like a hill, like the cliff it strikes, and the wave boils up from
below   240

verticibus nigramque alte subiectat harenam.

   Omne adeo genus in terris hominumque, ferarumque
et genus aequoreum, pecudes pictaeque volucres,
in furias ignemque ruunt: amor omnibus idem.

tempore non alio catulorum oblita leaena   245
saevior erravit campis, nec funera vulgo
tam multa informes ursi stragemque dedere
per silvas; tum saevus aper, tum pessima tigris;
heu male tum Libyae solis erratur in agris.

nonne vides ut tota tremor pertemptet equorum   250
corpora, si tantum notas odor attulit auras?
ac neque eos iam frena virum neque verbera saeva,
non scopuli rupesque cavae atque obiecta retardant
flumina correptosque unda torquentia montis.

ipse ruit dentesque Sabellicus exacuit sus,   255
et pede prosubigit terram, fricat arbore costas,
atque hinc atque illinc umeros ad vulnera durat.

quid iuvenis, magnum cui versat in ossibus ignem
durus amor? nempe abruptis turbata procellis
nocte natat caeca serus freta; quem super ingens   260
porta tonat caeli et scopulis inlisa reclamant
aequora; nec miseri possunt revocare parentes
nec moritura super crudeli funere virgo.

quid lynces Bacchi variae et genus acre luporum
atque canum? quid, quae imbelles dant proelia cervi?   265
scilicet ante omnis furor est insignis equarum;
et mentem Venus ipsa dedit, quo tempore Glauci
Potniades malis membra absumpsere quadrigae.

illas ducit amor trans Gargara transque sonantem

Eddying and hurls dark shingle high up along the shore.

All manner of life on earth—men, fauna of land and sea,
Cattle and coloured birds—
Run to this fiery madness: love is alike for all.
At no season but love's does the lioness so neglect   245
Her cubs and range so savage over the plain, or the clumsy
Bear deal out such wholesale death and destruction in the
     woods;
Then is the boar morose, the tigress in a wicked temper;
Ah, that's no time to be wandering alone through the Libyan
     desert!
Look how a horse shudders in his whole frame, if the
     familiar   250
Scent is but borne downwind!
Nothing will hold him now—neither bridle nor blows of the
     whip,
Not cliffs and cavernous rocks and watercourses that lie
In his path and whirl away mountains their spate undermines.
The famed Sabellian boar now whets his tusks and
     charges,   255
Tramples the ground before him, rubs his ribs against trees,
And makes a defensive armour of his shoulders on either flank.
Think of a young man, burning with cruel love to the bone:
Think of him, late in the blindfold night swimming the
     narrows
That are vexed by headlong gales, while above his head the
     huge   260
Gates of heaven thunder and the seas collide with a crash
Against the capes: powerless to recall him his sorrowful
     parents
And the girl who is soon to die of grief over his body.
Remember the Wine-god's lynxes, the rabid race of wolves
And hounds, and the way unwarlike stags will offer to
     fight.   265
But of all, beyond doubt, the fury of mares is the most re-
     markable:
Venus herself incited
The chariot-team that day they champed the limbs of
     Glaucus.
In heat, they'll range over Gargarus and across the roaring

Ascanium; superant montis et flumina tranant.   270
continuoque avidis ubi subdita flamma medullis
(vere magis, quia vere calor redit ossibus) illae
ore omnes versae ad Zephyrum stant rupibus altis,
exceptantque levis auras et saepe sine ullis
coniugiis vento gravidae—mirabile dictu—   275
saxa per et scopulos et depressas convallis
diffugiunt, non, Eure, tuos, neque solis ad ortus,
in Borean Caurumque, aut unde nigerrimus Auster
nascitur et pluvio contristat frigore caelum.
hic demum, hippomanes vero quod nomine dicunt   280
pastores, lentum destillat ab inguine virus,
hippomanes, quod saepe malae legere novercae
miscueruntque herbas et non innoxia verba.

   Sed fugit interea, fugit inreparabile tempus,
singula dum capti circumvectamur amore.   285
hoc satis armentis. superat pars altera curae,
lanigeros agitare greges hirtasque capellas.
hic labor, hinc laudem fortes sperate coloni.
nec sum animi dubius verbis ea vincere magnum
quam sit et angustis hunc addere rebus honorem;   290
sed me Parnasi deserta per ardua dulcis
raptat amor; iuvat ire iugis, qua nulla priorum
Castaliam molli devertitur orbita clivo.
nunc, veneranda Pales, magno nunc ore sonandum.

   Incipiens stabulis edico in mollibus herbam   295
carpere ovis, dum mox frondosa reducitur aestas,
et multa duram stipula filicumque maniplis
sternere subter humum, glacies ne frigida laedat
molle pecus scabiemque ferat turpisque podagras.

Ascanius, they'll climb mountains and swim rivers.   270
The moment that flame is kindled within their passionate
    flesh
(In spring above all, when warmth returns to their bones)
    the whole herd
Wheels to face the west wind high up there on the rocks;
They snuff the light airs and often without being mated
Conceive, for the wind—astounding to tell—impregnates
    them: 275
Over the rocks and cliffs then, and down the deep dales
They gallop scattering, not towards the east and the dayspring
But to the north and north-west
And where the south wind arises glooming the sky with cold
    rain.
Whereupon a clammy fluid, which herdsmen call   280
Correctly 'hippomanes', oozes from out their groin—
Hippomanes, by wicked stepmothers much sought after
And mixed with herbs and malignant cantrips to brew a spell.
    But time is on the move still, time that will not return,
While we go cruising around this subject whose lore delights
    us.   285
So much for herds. The second part of my work remains—
The business of wool-bearing flocks and shaggy she-goats.
Here's work for you, stalwart farmers, and a hope of winning
    fame.
I'm well aware it's hard to master this subject in words
And honour a theme so constricted: but over those steep
    and lonely   290
Places I'm winged by poetry's
Rapture: how grand to go on that ridge where no man before
    me
Has made his mark wheeling aside down the gentle slope!
Now, worshipful goddess of sheepfolds, grant me a fuller
    tone!
    To begin with, I prescribe that in their cosy pens   295
The sheep should feed till leafy summer's soon return;
And that you put down plenty of straw and bundles of
    bracken
On the hard ground, to guard your flock against the wintry
Frost which is apt to give them scab and the nasty foot-rot.

post hinc digressus iubeo frondentia capris   300
arbuta sufficere et fluvios praebere recentis,
et stabula a ventis hiberno opponere soli
ad medium conversa diem, cum frigidus olim
iam cadit extremoque inrorat Aquarius anno.
hae quoque non cura nobis leviore tuendae   305
(nec minor usus erit, quamvis Milesia magno
vellera mutentur Tyrios incocta rubores);
densior hinc suboles, hinc largi copia lactis;
quam magis exhausto spumaverit ubere mulctra,
laeta magis pressis manabunt flumina mammis.   310
nec minus interea barbas incanaque menta
Cinyphii tondent hirci saetasque comantis
usum in castrorum et miseris velamina nautis.
pascuntur vero silvas et summa Lycaei,
horrentisque rubos et amantis ardua dumos.   315
atque ipsae memores redeunt in tecta, suosque
ducunt, et gravido superant vix ubere limen.
ergo omni studio glaciem ventosque nivalis,
quo minor est illis curae mortalis egestas,
avertes, victumque feres et virgea laetus   320
pabula, nec tota claudes faenilia bruma.
at vero Zephyris cum laeta vocantibus aestas
in saltus utrumque gregem atque in pascua mittet,
Luciferi primo cum sidere frigida rura
carpamus, dum mane novum, dum gramina canent,   325
et ros in tenera pecori gratissimus herba.
inde ubi quarta sitim caeli collegerit hora
et cantu querulae rumpent arbusta cicadae,
ad puteos aut alta greges ad stagna iubebo
currentem ilignis potare canalibus undam;   330
aestibus at mediis umbrosam exquirere vallem,

Passing on, I suggest for the goats a stock of flowering   300
Arbutus, fresh stream-water,
And stalls sheltered from wind, facing the winter sun,
Turned towards the midday, at the time when cold Aquarius
Is setting and asperges the skirts of the dying year.
Goats require as careful looking-after as sheep   305
(Nor less will their profit be, although Milesian fleeces
Dyed in Tyrian purples fetch you an excellent price);
For their young are more numerous and their yield of milk is
          large;
The fuller the milk-pails foam from their exhausted udders,
The richer milk you'll get when you squeeze their teats
          again.   310
Besides, men clip the beard,
The grizzled chin and bristly coat of the Libyan he-goat,
For use in camps and to make sailcloth for luckless mariners.
Their pasture is an Arcadian forest or height, where they feed
On prickly brambles and on thorn-bushes that love a
          hillside.   315
Unherded they remember to come home, they lead their
          young,
Hardly lift their heavy udders through the half-door.
So take the more trouble, because their demands on human
          aid
Are less, to guard them from frosts and snowy winds, and to
          give them
Freely their keep and fodder   320
Of boughs, leaving your hayloft open throughout the winter.
But when the west winds call and the exquisite warm season
Ushers them out, both sheep and goats, to glade and pasture,
At the first wink of the Morning Star let us wend away
To the frore fields, while the morning is young, the meadow
          pearly,   325
And dew so dear to cattle lies on the tender grass.
Then, when the fourth hour of the sun has created a thirst
And the plantations vibrate with the pizzicato of crickets,
I'll bring the flocks to water by wells and by deep ponds,
I'll bid them drink the water that runs in the troughs of
          ilex.   330
But now it's the noonday heat, make for a shady combe

sicubi magna Iovis antiquo robore quercus
ingentis tendat ramos, aut sicubi nigrum
ilicibus crebris sacra nemus accubet umbra;
tum tenuis dare rursus aquas et pascere rursus   335
solis ad occasum, cum frigidus aëra vesper
temperat, et saltus reficit iam roscida luna,
litoraque alcyonen resonant, acalanthida dumi.

Quid tibi pastores Libyae, quid pascua versu
prosequar et raris habitata mapalia tectis?   340
saepe diem noctemque et totum ex ordine mensem
pascitur itque pecus longa in deserta sine ullis
hospitiis: tantum campi iacet. omnia secum
armentarius Afer agit, tectumque laremque
armaque Amyclaeumque canem Cressamque pharetram;   345
non secus ac patriis acer Romanus in armis
iniusto sub fasce viam cum carpit, et hosti
ante exspectatum positis stat in agmine castris.

At non qua Scythiae gentes Maeotiaque unda,
turbidus et torquens flaventis Hister harenas,   350
quaque redit medium Rhodope porrecta sub axem.
illic clausa tenent stabulis armenta, neque ullae
aut herbae campo apparent aut arbore frondes;
sed iacet aggeribus niveis informis et alto
terra gelu late septemque adsurgit in ulnas.   355
semper hiems, semper spirantes frigora Cauri.
tum Sol pallentis haud umquam discutit umbras,
nec cum invectus equis altum petit aethera, nec cum
praecipitem Oceani rubro lavit aequore currum.
concrescunt subitae currenti in flumine crustae,   360
undaque iam tergo ferratos sustinet orbis,

Where some great ancient-hearted oak throws out its huge
Boughs, or the wood is black with
A wealth of holm-oak and broods in its own haunted shadow.
Then give them runnels of water again and let them
    browse   335
About sundown, when the cool star of evening assuages
The air, and moonlight falls now with dew to freshen the
    glades,
And the kingfisher's heard on the shore and the warbler in
    woody thickets.
    Shall I tell you of African shepherds, describe to you in
    my verse
Their grazing-grounds and the scattered shanties wherein
    they dwell?   340
Daylong and nightlong often, yes, for a month on end
Their flocks go grazing into the desert distances
Where no habitation is, so broad stretches the plain.
The African herdsman takes everything with him—his hearth
    and home,
Weapons, hound and quiver: 345
Just so will the fierce Roman, armed as his fathers were,
Make a forced march, though carrying excessive weight of
    equipment,
Till the column is halted, the camp pitched, the foe surprised.
    Not so among the northern tribes by the Sea of Azof,
And where the Danube swirls muddy with yellow sand   350
Or beneath the mid-pole Mount Rhodope stretches to east
    and north.
The cattle are kept in the stalls there;
Not a blade of grass appears on the plain, not a leaf on the
    trees:
But far as eye can reach earth lies, her features lost
Beneath snowdrifts and ice to a depth of seven fathoms.   355
It's always winter, always the cold nor-wester blowing.
And worse, the sun can never break through the wan gloom
    there—
Not when his horses draw him up to the height of heaven,
Not when his chariot brings him to bathe in the blood-red sea.
Films of ice form suddenly over the flowing rivers;   360
And next, the water is bearing iron wheels on its back

puppibus illa prius, patulis nunc hospita plaustris;
aeraque dissiliunt vulgo, vestesque rigescunt
indutae, caeduntque securibus umida vina,
et totae solidam in glaciem vertere lacunae,   365
stiriaque impexis induruit horrida barbis.
interea toto non setius aëre ningit:
intereunt pecudes, stant circumfusa pruinis
corpora magna boum, confertoque agmine cervi
torpent mole nova et summis vix cornibus exstant.   370
hos non immissis canibus, non cassibus ullis
puniceaeve agitant pavidos formidine pennae,
sed frustra oppositum trudentis pectore montem
comminus obtruncant ferro, graviterque rudentis
caedunt, et magno laeti clamore reportant.   375
ipsi in defossis specubus secura sub alta
otia agunt terra, congestaque robora totasque
advolvere focis ulmos ignique dedere.
hic noctem ludo ducunt, et pocula laeti
fermento atque acidis imitantur vitea sorbis.   380
talis Hyperboreo septem subiecta trioni
gens effrena virum Riphaeo tunditur Euro
et pecudum fulvis velatur corpora saetis.
    Si tibi lanitium curae, primum aspera silva
lappaeque tribolique absint; fuge pabula laeta: 385
continuoque greges villis lege mollibus albos.
illum autem, quamvis aries sit candidus ipse,
nigra subest udo tantum cui lingua palato,
reice, ne maculis infuscet vellera pullis
nascentum, plenoque alium circumspice campo.   390
munere sic niveo lanae, si credere dignum est,

And harbours broad-beamed waggons, that once was a home
 for ships:
Brass vessels constantly burst, clothes freeze stiff as you wear
 them,
Wine can be chopped with an axe,
Whole tarns are turned to solid ice, and icicles grow 365
Bristling on uncombed beards.
All this while the air is one white drift of snow:
Cattle die, the bulky oxen stand about
Shrouded in frost, and herds of deer huddling together
Grow numb beneath new-formed drifts, their antlers barely
 showing. 370
Men hunt them not with hounds now, nor do they use the nets,
No scarlet-feathered toils are needed to break their nerve;
But the deer vainly shove at the banked-up snow with their
 shoulders,
The men attack them at close quarters, they cut them down
Belling loud, and cheerfully shout as they bring them
 home. 375
They themselves dig out deep igloos underground
Where they live in carefree leisure, keeping up their fire
With oak from the stack and trunks of elm they trundle to
 the hearth.
Here they while away the darkness in games, and gladly
Make do with beer and a rough cider for draughts of
 wine. 380
Such are the tameless tribes
Of the north, beneath the seven-starred Bear much buffeted
By east winds, wearing the tawny fur of beasts for protection.
 If wool-growing is your business, beware of barbed vege-
 tation,
Goose-grass and star-thistle: avoid too rich a grazing: 385
Choose from the start a flock both white and soft of fleece.
Reject any ram, however pure a white his wool,
If the tongue beneath his moist palate is black, for he'll breed
Lambs with black-spotted fleeces—
Reject, and look round for another ram on the crowded
 sheep-run. 390
With the lure of such snowy wool, if the legend is worth
 belief,

Pan deus Arcadiae captam te, Luna, fefellit
in nemora alta vocans; nec tu aspernata vocantem.

At cui lactis amor, cytisum lotosque frequentis
ipse manu salsasque ferat praesepibus herbas.   395
hinc et amant fluvios magis, et magis ubera tendunt
et salis occultum referunt in lacte saporem.
multi etiam excretos prohibent a matribus haedos
primaque ferratis praefigunt ora capistris.
quod surgente die mulsere horisque diurnis,   400
nocte premunt; quod iam tenebris et sole cadente,
sub lucem exportant calathis—adit oppida pastor—
aut parco sale contingunt hiemique reponunt.

Nec tibi cura canum fuerit postrema, sed una
velocis Spartae catulos acremque Molossum   405
pasce sero pingui. numquam custodibus illis
nocturnum stabulis furem incursusque luporum
aut impacatos a tergo horrebis Hiberos.
saepe etiam cursu timidos agitabis onagros,
et canibus leporem, canibus venabere dammas;   410
saepe volutabris pulsos silvestribus apros
latratu turbabis agens, montisque per altos
ingentem clamore premes ad retia cervum.

Disce et odoratam stabulis accendere cedrum,
galbaneoque agitare gravis nidore chelydros.   415
saepe sub immotis praesepibus aut mala tactu
vipera delituit caelumque exterrita fugit,
aut tecto adsuetus coluber succedere et umbrae
(pestis acerba boum) pecorique aspergere virus,

Pan, god of Arcady, captivated and tricked the Moon,
Calling her down to the deep woods—a call she disdained not.
> But the man who is out for milk should bring plenty of
> clover,
Trefoil and salted grass to the goat-pens, and do it in
person.   395
Since a thirst for water is whetted thus, and their udders
swell,
And they'll impart to the milk a faint sub-flavour of salt.
Many will even keep the new-born kids from their mothers
By fixing iron-spiked muzzles over the suckling mouths.
The milk they obtain at dawn or   400
During the day, they cheese at night: the evening milk
They pack off at dawn in frails and the shepherd takes it to
town,
Or sprinkle lightly with salt and put it by for the winter.
> Last but not least, the care of your dogs: let them feed
> together
On fattening whey—swift greyhound pups and alert mas-
tiffs.   405
You'll never need to fear
Robbers by night in your cattle-pens or a raid of wolves
Or Spanish brigands creeping behind you, while they're on
guard.
Often too men hunt the timid wild ass, the hare
And fallow deer with hounds: 410
Often again their barking will start a wild boar and drive him
From where he wallows in the wood; or in full cry they'll
hunt a
Noble stag over the uplands and manœuvre him towards the
nets.
> It's wise also to burn sweet juniper in the byres,
Rout out the fetid-smelling snakes with fumes of gum.   415
When stalls go long uncleaned, you'll commonly find beneath
them
A viper lurking, hater of light, unhealthy to touch;
Or the serpent, whose habit is to creep into dark corners of
buildings
(A damnable plague to oxen) and inject the herd with his
poison,

fovit humum. cape saxa manu, cape robora, pastor,   420
tollentemque minas et sibila colla tumentem
deice. iamque fuga timidum caput abdidit alte,
cum medii nexus extremaeque agmina caudae
solvuntur, tardosque trahit sinus ultimus orbis.
est etiam ille malus Calabris in saltibus anguis   425
squamea convolvens sublato pectore terga
atque notis longam maculosus grandibus alvum,
qui, dum amnes ulli rumpuntur fontibus et dum
vere madent udo terrae ac pluvialibus Austris,
stagna colit, ripisque habitans hic piscibus atram   430
improbus ingluviem ranisque loquacibus explet;
postquam exusta palus, terraeque ardore dehiscunt,
exsilit in siccum, et flammantia lumina torquens
saevit agris, asperque siti atque exterritus aestu.
ne mihi tum mollis sub divo carpere somnos   435
neu dorso nemoris libeat iacuisse per herbas,
cum positis novus exuviis nitidusque iuventa
volvitur, aut catulos tectis aut ova relinquens,
arduus ad solem, et linguis micat ore trisulcis.

　　Morborum quoque te causas et signa docebo.   440
turpis ovis temptat scabies, ubi frigidus imber
altius ad vivum persedit et horrida cano
bruma gelu, vel cum tonsis inlotus adhaesit
sudor et hirsuti secuerunt corpora vepres.
dulcibus idcirco fluviis pecus omne magistri   445
perfundunt, udisque aries in gurgite villis
mersatur missusque secundo defluit amni;
aut tonsum tristi contingunt corpus amurca
et spumas miscent argenti vivaque sulpura
Idaeasque pices et pinguis unguine ceras   450
scillamque elleborosque gravis nigrumque bitumen.

Lies lodged in earth. Take stones, shepherd, take a stick and
    strike   420
Him down as he rears in malice, hissing, his neck puffed out.
He's hidden his cowardly head now
In the hole; his middle folds and the writhing tip of his tail
Unwind, as the last coil slithers away slowly.
Or take that evil watersnake of Calabrian woods   425
Who bowls around with upright port; his back is scaly,
His belly long and marked all over in big blotches:
That one, while streams are still issuing from their source
And earth remains dank with the wet spring and the rainy
    south wind,
Living in ponds, housekeeping on river-banks, will cram
    his   430
Black maw with fish and garrulous frogs immoderately.
But when the swamp dries out and a hot sun splits the earth
He darts onto dry land, rolling his flame-shot eyes,
And raves through the meadows, mad with thirst, crazy with
    heat.
I only hope I shall never be tempted to sleep in the open   435
Or repose on a forest ridge
Among the grass, when that one has cast his slough and
    glides out
Gleaming in youth, leaving his young or his eggs at home,
Erect to the sun, forked tongue flickering between his lips.
    Diseases too will I treat of—their causes, signs and
    symptoms.   440
Rotting mange afflicts a flock when chilly rain
And hoar-frost of midwinter work deep into the living
Flesh, or when the sheep have been sheared and clotted
    sweat
Clings to their unwashed bodies and tangles of briar have
    cut them.
As a remedy, the whole flock is dipped in running water   445
By the flock-masters, the ram plunged in a pool to soak
His fleece and float downstream;
Or the shorn bodies are smeared with bitter olive-lees,
And a salve is compounded of silver oxide, native sulphur,
Pitch, emollient wax-paste,   450
Squills and stinking hellebore and black bitumen:

non tamen ulla magis praesens fortuna laborum est
quam si quis ferro potuit rescindere summum
ulceris os; alitur vitium vivitque tegendo,
dum medicas adhibere manus ad vulnera pastor   455
abnegat et meliora deos sedet omnia poscens.
quin etiam, ima dolor balantum lapsus ad ossa
cum furit atque artus depascitur arida febris,
profuit incensos aestus avertere et inter
ima ferire pedis salientem sanguine venam,   460
Bisaltae quo more solent acerque Gelonus,
cum fugit in Rhodopen atque in deserta Getarum
et lac concretum cum sanguine potat equino.
quam procul aut molli succedere saepius umbrae
videris, aut summas carpentem ignavius herbas   465
extremamque sequi, aut medio procumbere campo
pascentem et serae solam decedere nocti,
continuo culpam ferro compesce, priusquam
dira per incautum serpant contagia vulgus.
non tam creber agens hiemem ruit aequore turbo   470
quam multae pecudum pestes. nec singula morbi
corpora corripiunt, sed tota aestiva repente,
spemque gregemque simul cunctamque ab origine gentem.
tum sciat, aërias Alpis et Norica si quis
castella in tumulis et Iapydis arva Timavi   475
nunc quoque post tanto videat, desertaque regna
pastorum et longe saltus lateque vacantis.

   Hic quondam morbo caeli miseranda coorta est
tempestas, totoque autumni incanduit aestu,
et genus omne neci pecudum dedit, omne ferarum,   480
corrupitque lacus, infecit pabula tabo.
nec via mortis erat simplex: sed ubi ignea venis

Though indeed there's no better method of inducing in this
    disease
A favourable crisis than to cut away with a knife
The putrid place; for the malady lives and thrives by con-
    cealment,
As long as the shepherd, unwilling to lay a hand on the
    wound   455
And heal it, merely sits back and prays for some improvement.
Further, when pain courses through bone and marrow of the
    bleating
Flock and a dry fever is wasting their limbs away,
It's well to bleed the artery that throbs in their hoof, and thus
Reduce the rage of the fever: 460
That's what the Macedonians do and the tough Gelonians,
Migrating to Rhodope or the wastes by the river Danube—
Men who drink their milk curdled with horses' blood.
If you notice from far one sheep more often seeking the
    shade's
Comfort, cropping the top of the grass more languidly,   465
Lagging behind the rest, lying down in the middle of the
    meadow
Where it grazes, and going off by itself as night descends,
You must nip that evil in the bud, you must use your knife
    and kill
Before its dread contagion creeps through the oblivious flock.
Thicker and faster than squalls of wind that tear at the sea's
    face   470
Come many diseases of cattle,
Killing not one here and there, but a whole summer pasture—
The lambs, the dams, the whole lot of them root and branch.
You'd bear me out, if you went to look at the lofty Alps,
The hill forts of Bavaria, the fields beside Timavo;   475
It happened long ago here, but you'd see the derelict ranches
Of sheep, old grazings empty up to the far horizon.

    For here it was that once the sky fell sick and a doleful
Season came, all hectic with the close heat of autumn,
And it killed off the whole gamut of cattle and wild
    beasts,   480
Infected their drinking pools and put a blight on their fodder.
Death took them by two stages:

omnibus acta sitis miseros adduxerat artus,
rursus abundabat fluidus liquor omniaque in se
ossa minutatim morbo conlapsa trahebat.   485
saepe in honore deum medio stans hostia ad aram,
lanea dum nivea circumdatur infula vitta,
inter cunctantis cecidit moribunda ministros.
aut si quam ferro mactaverat ante sacerdos,
inde neque impositis ardent altaria fibris,   490
nec responsa potest consultus reddere vates,
ac vix suppositi tinguntur sanguine cultri
summaque ieiuna sanie infuscatur harena.
hinc laetis vituli vulgo moriuntur in herbis
et dulcis animas plena ad praesepia reddunt;   495
hinc canibus blandis rabies venit, et quatit aegros
tussis anhela sues ac faucibus angit obesis.
labitur infelix studiorum atque immemor herbae
victor equus fontisque avertitur et pede terram
crebra ferit; demissae aures, incertus ibidem   500
sudor et ille quidem morituris frigidus: aret
pellis et ad tactum tractanti dura resistit.
haec ante exitium primis dant signa diebus.
sin in processu coepit crudescere morbus,
tum vero ardentes oculi atque attractus ab alto   505
spiritus, interdum gemitu gravis, imaque longo
ilia singultu tendunt, it naribus ater
sanguis, et obsessas fauces premit aspera lingua.
profuit inserto latices infundere cornu
Lenaeos; ea visa salus morientibus una.   510

When parching thirst had seared the veins and shrivelled
    the poor limbs,
Watery humours broke out again in flux till the bones all
Rotted and melted piecemeal as the malady ran its
    course.   485
Often a victim, brought to the altar for sacrifice,
At the moment they placed the white-ribboned tiara of wool
    upon it
Fell down dying among them, while the acolytes delayed.
Or, if the priest had killed in time, he could not kindle
To flame the filaments laid on the altar, nor could the
    seer   490
Make any sense of them:
The knife beneath the throat was barely stained with blood,
A meagre trickle of bloody matter just tinged the sand.
Now over the rank pasture calves are dying by droves,
Gasping out their life amid the abundant mangers: 495
Now rabies comes to good-tempered dogs; a painful cough
Racks the sick swine, and their throats swell and they
    suffocate.
The horse, a prize-winner once, takes no more pride in his
    paces,
Forgets the grass, turns away from water, keeps on stamping
The ground; sweat comes and goes on his dejected
    ears—   500
A cold sweat meaning death:
The hide feels dry if you stroke him, stubborn and harsh to
    the touch.
Such are the earlier signs he gives of a mortal sickness.
But when the disease begins to reach a deadlier stage,
The eyes are inflamed, the breath comes deep and dragging,
    broken   505
By heavy groans, the long flanks heave with profound sobs,
Out of the nostrils oozes
Black blood, the tongue is rough and swells in the throat and
    blocks it.
Some use it was to insert a drenching-horn and give them
Wine: it seemed the one thing that would restore the
    dying.   510

mox erat hoc ipsum exitio, furiisque refecti
ardebant ipsique suos iam morte sub aegra
(di meliora piis, erroremque hostibus illum!).
discissos nudis laniabant dentibus artus.
ecce autem duro fumans sub vomere taurus   515
concidit et mixtum spumis vomit ore cruorem
extremosque ciet gemitus. it tristis arator
maerentem abiungens fraterna morte iuvencum,
atque opere in medio defixa relinquit aratra.
non umbrae altorum nemorum, non mollia possunt   520
prata movere animum, non qui per saxa volutus
purior electro campum petit amnis; at ima
solvuntur latera, atque oculos stupor urget inertis,
ad terramque fluit devexo pondere cervix.
quid labor aut benefacta iuvant? quid vomere terras   525
invertisse gravis? atqui non Massica Bacchi
munera, non illis epulae nocuere repostae:
frondibus et victu pascuntur simplicis herbae,
pocula sunt fontes liquidi atque exercita cursu
flumina, nec somnos abrumpit cura salubris.   530
    tempore non alio dicunt regionibus illis
quaesitas ad sacra boves Iunonis et uris
imparibus ductos alta ad donaria currus.
ergo aegre rastris terram rimantur, et ipsis
unguibus infodiunt fruges, montisque per altos   535
contenta cervice trahunt stridentia plaustra.
non lupus insidias explorat ovilia circum
nec gregibus nocturnus obambulat: acrior illum
cura domat; timidi dammae cervique fugaces
nunc interque canes et circum tecta vagantur.   540

But soon this remedy proved fatal, the sick revived
Only to rave in madness till under the mortal plague
(God send something better to good men, and leave to our
    foes that error!)
Teeth bared, they savaged their own limbs and tore them-
    selves to shreds.
Watch that bull, steaming from the weight of the iron
    coulter!   515
He drops in his tracks, his mouth drools with a bloody foam,
A last groan lifts to heaven. Sadly the ploughman goes
To unyoke the bullock mourning his butty's death: the plough
Stays there, stuck in the middle of the field they never
    finished.
No tall trees' shade, no gentle   520
Meads will console the beast, no becks brighter than amber
Scampering down over rocks to the plain: relaxed and flabby
Grow the long flanks, listless and dazed the downcast eye,
Slowly the neck droops dispirited to the ground.
He toiled for us and served us, he turned the difficult
    earth   525
With the plough,—and what does it profit him? Yet these
    were never
Drinkers of wine, nor harmed their health by incessant
    banquets:
No, their diet is leaves and simple grass alone,
Their cup is the clear springs
And hurrying streams, no cares disquiet their healthy
    sleep.   530
    At no other time, or so they tell us, in those parts
Were oxen rarely obtained for Juno's rites, and chariots
Hauled to high votive-shrines by ill-matched buffalo teams.
Painfully men scratched at the soil with mattocks, used their
Own nails to cover in the seed corn, harnessed their
    necks   535
To tug the creaking waggons over a towering hillside.
Wolves lurk no longer in ambush around the folds, nor lope
Towards the flock at night: more desperate their affairs
And make them tame. Now timid fallow-deer and elusive
Stags wander amongst the hounds and about men's
    houses.   540

iam maris immensi prolem et genus omne natantum
litore in extremo, ceu naufraga corpora fluctus
proluit; insolitae fugiunt in flumina phocae.
interit et curvis frustra defensa latebris
vipera et attoniti squamis astantibus hydri. 545
ipsis est aër avibus non aequus, et illae
praecipites alta vitam sub nube relinquunt.
praeterea iam nec mutari pabula refert,
quaesitaeque nocent artes; cessere magistri,
Phillyrides Chiron Amythaoniusque Melampus. 550
saevit et in lucem Stygiis emissa tenebris
pallida Tisiphone Morbos agit ante Metumque,
inque dies avidum surgens caput altius effert.
balatu pecorum et crebris mugitibus amnes
arentesque sonant ripae collesque supini. 555
iamque catervatim dat stragem atque aggerat ipsis
in stabulis turpi dilapsa cadavera tabo,
donec humo tegere ac foveis abscondere discunt.
nam neque erat coriis usus, nec viscera quisquam
aut undis abolere potest aut vincere flamma; 560
ne tondere quidem morbo inluvieque peresa
vellera nec telas possunt attingere putris;
verum etiam invisos si quis temptaret amictus,
ardentes papulae atque immundus olentia sudor
membra sequebatur, nec longo deinde moranti 565
tempore contactos artus sacer ignis edebat.

Now the deepwater tribes, yes, all the swimming creatures
Lie on the shore's edge, washed by the waves like ship-
    wrecked bodies
And seals take refuge in rivers they never swam before.
The viper perishes too, in vain defence of her winding
Lair; and the startled snake, his scales standing on end.   545
The air's precarious even for birds; they plunge down dead,
Leaving their life in the clouds.
Beside all this, changes of diet achieved nothing,
Cures they invented only killed; healers gave up—
Chiron son of Phillyra, Amythaon's son Melampus.   550
From hell's black country came the pale Tisiphone raging
Into broad daylight, fear and plague galloped on before her,
Higher and hungrier rose her head day after day.
Bleatings and mooings went up, a multitudinous cry,
From streams, parched river-banks and all the prostrate
    hills.   555
And now they died by whole companies, and the corpses
Rotting with vile decay lay piled in the very sheep-folds,
Till men had learnt to put them in pits, covered with earth.
The hide was no good, and no man
Could cleanse the carcase in water or burn it up with
    fire: 560
You could not even shear the fleece, it was so corroded
With the foul pus, or work that rotten wool in the loom:
But if you were so foolhardy as to wear the hideous garment,
Inflamed pustules and a noxious-smelling sweat appeared
All over your limbs: not long then   565
Before the fiery curse ate up your tettered frame.

LIBER IV

Protinus aërii mellis caelestia dona
exsequar. hanc etiam, Maecenas, aspice partem.
admiranda tibi levium spectacula rerum—
magnanimosque duces totiusque ordine gentis
mores et studia et populos et proelia dicam.   5
in tenui labor; at tenuis non gloria, si quem
numina laeva sinunt auditque vocatus Apollo.
    Principio sedes apibus statioque petenda,
quo neque sit ventis aditus (nam pabula venti
ferre domum prohibent), neque oves haedique petulci   10
floribus insultent, aut errans bucula campo
decutiat rorem et surgentis atterat herbas.
absint et picti squalentia terga lacerti
pinguibus a stabulis, meropesque aliaeque volucres,
et manibus Procne pectus signata cruentis;   15
omnia nam late vastant ipsasque volantis
ore ferunt dulcem nidis immitibus escam.
at liquidi fontes et stagna virentia musco
adsint et tenuis fugiens per gramina rivus,
palmaque vestibulum aut ingens oleaster inumbret,   20
ut, cum prima novi ducent examina reges
vere suo, ludetque favis emissa iuventus,
vicina invitet decedere ripa calori

BOOK 4

Next I come to the manna, the heavenly gift of honey.
Look kindly on this part too, my friend. I'll tell of a tiny
Republic that makes a show well worth your admiration—
Great-hearted leaders, a whole nation whose work is planned,
Their morals, groups, defences—I'll tell you in due order.   5
A featherweight theme: but one that can load me with fame,
     if only
No wicked fairy cross me, and the Song-god come to my call.
   For a start you must find your bees a suitable home, a
     position
Sheltered from wind (for wind will stop them carrying
     home
Their forage), a close where sheep nor goats come butting
     in   10
To jump on the flowers, nor blundering heifer stray to flick
The dew from the meadow and stamp its springing grasses
     down.
Discourage the lizard, too, with his lapis-lazuli back,
From their rich folds, the bee-eater and other birds,
And the swallow whose breast was blooded once by a killer's
     hand: 15
For these wreak wholesale havoc, snap up your bees on the
     wing
And bear them off as a tit-bit for their ungentle nestlings.
But mind there's a bubbling spring nearby, a pool moss-
     bordered,
And a rill ghosting through the grass:
See, too, that a palm or tall oleaster shadow the entrance,   20
For thus, when the new queens lead out the earliest swarms—
The spring all theirs—and the young bees play, from hive
     unprisoned,
The bank may be handy to welcome them in out of the heat

obviaque hospitiis teneat frondentibus arbos.
in medium, seu stabit iners seu profluet umor,   25
transversas salices et grandia conice saxa,
pontibus ut crebris possint consistere et alas
pandere ad aestivum solem, si forte morantis
sparserit aut praeceps Neptuno immerserit Eurus.
haec circum casiae virides et olentia late   30
serpylla et graviter spirantis copia thymbrae
floreat, inriguumque bibant violaria fontem.
    ipsa autem, seu corticibus tibi suta cavatis
seu lento fuerint alvaria vimine texta,
angustos habeant aditus: nam frigore mella   35
cogit hiems, eademque calor liquefacta remittit.
utraque vis apibus pariter metuenda; neque illae
nequiquam in tectis certatim tenuia cera
spiramenta linunt, fucoque et floribus oras
explent, collectumque haec ipsa ad munera gluten   40
et visco et Phrygiae servant pice lentius Idae.
saepe etiam effossis, si vera est fama, latebris
sub terra fodere larem, penitusque repertae
pumicibusque cavis exesaeque arboris antro.
tu tamen et levi rimosa cubilia limo   45
ungue fovens circum, et raras superinice frondes.
neu propius tectis taxum sine, neve rubentis
ure foco cancros, altae neu crede paludi,
aut ubi odor caeni gravis aut ubi concava pulsu
saxa sonant vocisque offensa resultat imago.   50
    Quod superest, ubi pulsam hiemem Sol aureus egit
sub terras caelumque aestiva luce reclusit,

And the tree meet them halfway and make them at home in
    its foliage.
Whether the water flows or is stagnant, fling in the middle   25
Willow boughs criss-cross and big stones,
That the bees may have plenty of bridges to stand on and
    dry their wings
At the summer sun, in case a shower has caught them
    loitering
Or a gust of east wind ducked them suddenly in the water.
Green spurge-laurel should grow round about, wild thyme
    that perfumes   30
The air, masses of savory rich-breathing, and violet beds
Sucking the channelled stream.

    Now for the hive itself. Remember, whether you make it
By stitching concave bark or weaving tough withies together,
To give it a narrow doorway: for winter grips and freezes   35
The honey, and summer's melting heat runs it off to waste.
Either extreme is feared by the bees. It is not for fun
That they're so keen on caulking with wax the draughty
    chinks
In their roof, and stuff the rim of their hive with flowery
    pollen,
Storing up for this very job a glue they have gathered   40
Stickier than bird-lime or pitch from Anatolia.
Often too, if reports are true, they dig deep shelters
Underground and keep house there, or out of the way are
    found
In a sandstone hollow or the heart of a rotten tree.
None the less, you should smear with smooth mud their
    chinky chambers   45
Solicitously for warmth, and lay a thin dressing of leaves.
Don't have a yew too close to their house, or burn in a
    brazier
Reddening crab-shells: never risk them near a bog,
Or where there's a stink of mud, or a rock formation echoes
Hollow when struck and returns your voice like a ghostly
    reflection.   50

    For the rest, when the golden sun has driven winter to
    ground
And opened up all the leagues of the sky in summer light,

illae continuo saltus silvasque peragrant
purpureosque metunt flores et flumina libant
summa leves. hinc nescio qua dulcedine laetae 55
progeniem nidosque fovent, hinc arte recentis
excudunt ceras et mella tenacia fingunt.
hinc ubi iam emissum caveis ad sidera caeli
nare per aestatem liquidam suspexeris agmen
obscuramque trahi vento mirabere nubem, 60
contemplator: aquas dulcis et frondea semper
tecta petunt. huc tu iussos asperge sapores,
trita melisphylla et cerinthae ignobile gramen,
tinnitusque cie et Matris quate cymbala circum:
ipsae considunt medicatis sedibus, ipsae 65
intima more suo sese in cunabula condent.

   Sin autem ad pugnam exierint—nam saepe duobus
regibus incessit magno discordia motu,
continuoque animos vulgi et trepidantia bello
corda licet longe praesciscere: namque morantis 70
Martius ille aeris rauci canor increpat, et vox
auditur fractos sonitus imitata tubarum;
tum trepidae inter se coeunt pennisque coruscant
spiculaque exacuunt rostris aptantque lacertos,
et circa regem atque ipsa ad praetoria densae 75
miscentur magnisque vocant clamoribus hostem.
ergo ubi ver nactae sudum camposque patentis,
erumpunt portis; concurritur, aethere in alto
fit sonitus, magnum mixtae glomerantur in orbem
praecipitesque cadunt; non densior aëre grando 80
nec de concussa tantum pluit ilice glandis.

Over the glades and woodlands at once they love to wander
And suck the shining flowers and delicate sip the streams.
Sweet then is their strange delight   55
As they cherish their children, their nestlings: then with
      craftsmanship they
Hammer out the fresh wax and mould the tacky honey.
Then, as you watch the swarm bursting from hive and heaven-
      ward
Soaring, and floating there on the limpid air of summer—
A vague and wind-warped column of cloud to your wonder-
      ing eyes:—   60
Notice them, how they always make for fresh water and
      leafy
Shelter. Here you shall sprinkle fragrances to their taste—
Crushed balm, honeywort humble—
Make a tinkling noise round about and clash the Mother-
      god's cymbals.
They will settle down of their own accord in the place you
      have perfumed,   65
And crawl to the innermost room for rest, as their custom is.
   But now, suppose they have sallied to battle: for between
Two queens there often arises trouble that comes to war.
At once, from afar, forewarned you will be of the mob's
      anger,
Their hearts spoiling for a fight: 70
Martial, a brazen harshness, a roar rebuking the laggard
You hear, and a cry that is like the abrupt blasts of a trumpet.
Then, all agog, their wings quivering, they come together,
Stings are sharpened on beaks, sinews braced for action,
And around the queen in their hordes, right up to the queen's
      headquarters   75
They demonstrate, they challenge the foe with fearsome
      shouts.
So, on a dry spring day, when the sky's prairies are open,
They deploy from their gates, they charge together, in
      heaven's height
There's a din; they meet and scrimmage, forming a monster
      ball, and
Headlong they tumble down, thicker than hail in the air   80
Or a shower of acorns raining down from a shaken oak.

ipsi per medias acies insignibus alis
ingentis animos angusto in pectore versant,
usque adeo obnixi non cedere dum gravis aut hos
aut hos versa fuga victor dare terga subegit.   85
hi motus animorum atque haec certamina tanta
pulveris exigui iactu compressa quiescent.

　　Verum ubi ductores acie revocaveris ambo,
deterior qui visus, eum, ne prodigus obsit,
dede neci; melior vacua sine regnet in aula.   90
alter erit maculis auro squalentibus ardens;
nam duo sunt genera: hic melior, insignis et ore
et rutilis clarus squamis; ille horridus alter
desidia, latamque trahens inglorius alvum.
ut binae regum facies, ita corpora plebis.   95
namque aliae turpes horrent, ceu pulvere ab alto
cum venit et sicco terram spuit ore viator
aridus; elucent aliae et fulgore coruscant,
ardentes auro et paribus lita corpora guttis.
haec potior suboles, hinc caeli tempore certo   100
dulcia mella premes, nec tantum dulcia quantum
et liquida et durum Bacchi domitura saporem.
At cum incerta volant caeloque examina ludunt
contemnuntque favos et frigida tecta relinquunt,
instabilis animos ludo prohibebis inani.   105
nec magnus prohibere labor: tu regibus alas
eripe; non illis quisquam cunctantibus altum
ire iter aut castris audebit vellere signa.
invitent croceis halantes floribus horti
et custos furum atque avium cum falce saligna   110
Hellespontiaci servet tutela Priapi.

Illustrious of wing, through the battle-line the monarchs
Move, vast passions agitating their little breasts,
Obstinate not to give in till superior weight of numbers
Has forced one side or the other to turn their backs in
flight. 85
And all these epic battles and turbulent hearts you can silence
By flinging a handful of dust.

But, when you have recalled both the leaders from combat,
The one that appears worsted you must kill, lest she prove
a waste
And a nuisance, and let the winner be absolute in the
kingdom. 90
The one will be all aglow in golden-patined mail—
Two kinds there are—this one is the better, taking the eye
With her form and the flash of her shining scales; that other
is shaggy
From laziness, a low and pot-bellied crawler, a bad lot.
As the two queens differ in aspect, so in physique their
subjects. 95
For some are unkempt and squalid, like a traveller when he
comes
Athirst off a dusty road and spits the grit from his dry mouth;
While others gleam and glitter,
Their bodies perfectly marked in a pattern of shining gold.
These are the better breed: from these at the right
season 100
Sweet honey you'll get—not sweet so much as pure, and fit
To soften your wine's harsh flavour.
But when the swarms fly aimlessly and sport in the sky,
Looking down on their combs, leaving the hives to cool,
You must put a stop to this empty and irresponsible play. 105
It is not hard to stop.
Tear off the wings of their queens: while these wait on the
ground,
No bee will dare to leave his base or take off for a flight.
Let gardens breathing a scent of yellow flowers allure
them:
Let the god of gardens, who watches for birds and robbers,
keep them 110
Safe with his hook of willow.

ipse thymum pinosque ferens de montibus altis
tecta serat late circum cui talia curae;
ipse labore manum duro terat, ipse feracis
figat humo plantas et amicos inriget imbris.   115

  Atque equidem, extremo ni iam sub fine laborum
vela traham et terris festinem advertere proram,
forsitan et pinguis hortos quae cura colendi
ornaret canerem, biferique rosaria Paesti,
quoque modo potis gauderent intiba rivis   120
et virides apio ripae, tortusque per herbam
cresceret in ventrem cucumis; nec sera comantem
narcissum aut flexi tacuissem vimen acanthi
pallentisque hederas et amantis litora myrtos.
namque sub Oebaliae memini me turribus arcis,   125
qua niger umectat flaventia culta Galaesus,
Corycium vidisse senem, cui pauca relicti
iugera ruris erant, nec fertilis illa iuvencis
nec pecori opportuna seges nec commoda Baccho.
hic rarum tamen in dumis olus albaque circum   130
lilia verbenasque premens vescumque papaver,
regum aequabat opes animis, seraque revertens
nocte domum dapibus mensas onerabat inemptis.
primus vere rosam atque autumno carpere poma,
et cum tristis hiems etiamnum frigore saxa   135
rumperet et glacie cursus frenaret aquarum,
ille comam mollis iam tondebat hyacinthi
aestatem increpitans seram Zephyrosque morantis.
ergo apibus fetis idem atque examine multo
primus abundare et spumantia cogere pressis   140

The bee-keeper for his part should fetch down thyme and
    pine
From the hills above, and plant them broadly around the
    bees' home:
His hands should grow work-hardened, bedding the soil
    with fertile
Shoots, watering them well.   115
  Indeed, were it not that already my work has made its
    landfall
And I shorten sail and eagerly steer for the harbour mouth,
I'd sing perhaps of rich gardens, their planning and cul-
    tivation,
The rose beds of Paestum that blossom twice in a year,
The way endive rejoices to drink from a rivulet,   120
The bank all green with celery, the cucumber snaking
Amid the grass and swelling to greatness: I'd not forget
Late-flowering narcissus or gum-arabic's ringlet shoots,
Pale ivy, shore-loving myrtle.
I remember once beneath the battlements of Oebalia,   125
Where dark Galaesus waters the golden fields of corn,
I saw an old man, a Corycian, who owned a few poor acres
Of land once derelict, useless for arable,
No good for grazing, unfit for the cultivation of vines.
But he laid out a kitchen garden in rows amid the brush-
    wood,   130
Bordering it with white lilies, verbena, small-seeded poppy.
He was happy there as a king. He could go indoors at night
To a table heaped with dainties he never had to buy.
His first rose of spring, the earliest apples in autumn:
And when grim winter still was splitting the rocks with
    cold   135
And holding the watercourses with curb of ice, already
That man would be cutting his soft-haired hyacinths, com-
    plaining
Of summer's backwardness and the west winds slow to
    come.
His bees were the first to breed,
Enriching him with huge swarms: he squeezed the frothy
    honey   140

mella favis; illi tiliae atque uberrima pinus,
quotque in flore novo pomis se fertilis arbos
induerat, totidem autumno matura tenebat.
ille etiam seras in versum distulit ulmos
eduramque pirum et spinos iam pruna ferentis   145
iamque ministrantem platanum potantibus umbras.
verum haec ipse equidem spatiis exclusus iniquis
praetereo atque aliis post me memoranda relinquo.

    Nunc age, naturas apibus quas Iuppiter ipse
addidit expediam, pro qua mercede canoros   150
Curetum sonitus crepitantiaque aera secutae
Dictaeo caeli regem pavere sub antro.
solae communis natos, consortia tecta
urbis habent, magnisque agitant sub legibus aevum,
et patriam solae et certos novere penatis;   155
venturaeque hiemis memores aestate laborem
experiuntur et in medium quaesita reponunt.
namque aliae victu invigilant et foedere pacto
exercentur agris; pars intra saepta domorum
narcissi lacrimam et lentum de cortice gluten   160
prima favis ponunt fundamina, deinde tenacis
suspendunt ceras; aliae spem gentis adultos
educunt fetus; aliae purissima mella
stipant et liquido distendunt nectare cellas.
sunt, quibus ad portas cecidit custodia sorti,   165
inque vicem speculantur aquas et nubila caeli,
aut onera accipiunt venientum, aut agmine facto
ignavum fucos pecus a praesepibus arcent.
fervet opus, redolentque thymo fragrantia mella.

Before anyone else from the combs: he had limes and a
    wealth of pine trees:
And all the early blossom, that clothed his trees with promise
Of an apple crop, by autumn had come to maturity.
He had a gift, too, for transplanting in rows the far-grown
    elm,
The hardwood pear, the blackthorn bearing its weight of
    sloes,   145
And the plane that already offered a pleasant shade for
    drinking.
But these are matters the strict scope of my theme forbids
    me:
I must pass them by, and leave them for later men to enlarge
    on.
  Well then, let me speak of the natural gifts that God
    himself
Bestowed on the bees, their reward   150
For obeying the charms—the chorus and clashing brass of
    the priests—
And feeding the king of heaven when he hid in that Cretan
    cave,
They alone have their children in common, a city united
Beneath one roof and a life under established laws:
They know a native country, are sure of hearth and
    home.   155
Aware that winter is coming, they use the summer days
For work, and put their winnings into a common pool.
Some are employed in getting food, and by fixed agreement
Work on the fields: some stay within their fenced abode,
With tear of daffodil and gummy resin of tree-bark   160
Laying the first foundation of the honeycomb, then hanging
The stickfast wax: others bring up the young bees, the hope
Of their people: others press
The pure honey and cram the cells with that crystal nectar.
Some, allotted the duty of sentry-go at the gates,   165
Keep an eye out for showers and a sign of clouds in heaven,
Relieve incoming bees of their burden, or closing ranks
Shoo the drones—that work-shy gang—away from the bee-
    folds.
The work goes on like wildfire, the honey smells of thyme.

ac veluti lentis Cyclopes fulmina massis   170
cum properant, alii taurinis follibus auras
accipiunt redduntque, alii stridentia tingunt
aera lacu; gemit impositis incudibus Aetna;
illi inter sese magna vi bracchia tollunt
in numerum, versantque tenaci forcipe ferrum.   175
non aliter, si parva licet componere magnis,
Cecropias innatus apes amor urget habendi
munere quamque suo. grandaevis oppida curae
et munire favos et daedala fingere tecta.
at fessae multa referunt se nocte minores,   180
crura thymo plenae; pascuntur et arbuta passim
et glaucas salices casiamque crocumque rubentem
et pinguem tiliam et ferrugineos hyacinthos.
omnibus una quies operum, labor omnibus unus:
mane ruunt portis; nusquam mora; rursus easdem   185
vesper ubi e pastu tandem decedere campis
admonuit, tum tecta petunt, tum corpora curant;
fit sonitus mussantque oras et limina circum.
post, ubi iam thalamis se composuere, siletur
in noctem, fessosque sopor suus occupat artus.   190
nec vero a stabulis pluvia impendente recedunt
longius, aut credunt caelo adventantibus Euris:
sed circum tutae sub moenibus urbis aquantur,
excursusque brevis temptant, et saepe lapillos,
ut cumbae instabiles fluctu iactante saburram,   195
tollunt, his sese per inania nubila librant.
    illum adeo placuisse apibus mirabere morem,
quod neque concubitu indulgent, nec corpora segnes

Thus when the Blacksmith Giants work double shifts to
    forge   170
Thunderbolts out of the stubborn ore, some ply the bellows
Of bull-skin, and others plunge the hissing metal in troughs:
And while Mount Aetna moans beneath their anvils' stress
They raise their arms with the powerful alternate rhythm of
    cranks,
They keep the iron turning in the close grip of their
    tongs.   175
So, to compare small things
With great, an inborn love of possession impels the bees
Each to his own office. The old are the town's wardens,
Who wall the honeycombs and frame the intricate houses.
Tired, as the night deepens, the young return from
    labour,   180
Their legs laden with thyme: they feed afar on the arbute,
The silvery willow, the spurge laurel, the fire-blush saffron,
The lime blossom so rich, the rust-red martagon lily.
For one and all one work-time, and a like rest from work.
At morning they hurry from the hives, all helter-skelter:
    again,   185
When the Evening Star has told them to leave their meadow
    pasture,
They make for home, they refresh themselves. What a mur-
    muring
You hear as they drone around their policies and doorsteps!
Later, they settle down in their cells for the night, a silence
Falls, a drowsy fatigue falls.   190
If rain threatens, be sure they'll not roam too far afield
From their hives: they mistrust the sky, should an east wind
    be due:
At such times safely beneath the walls of their town they
    forage
Around, making brief excursions, and often carry some
    ballast,
As dinghies do to stiffen them in a high sea—they lift   195
Wee stones, and with these they weather the cloud-tossed
    solitudes.
    Most you shall marvel at this habit peculiar to bees—
That they have no sexual union: their bodies never dissolve

in Venerem solvunt aut fetus nixibus edunt;
verum ipsae e foliis natos, e suavibus herbis   200
ore legunt, ipsae regem parvosque Quirites
sufficiunt, aulasque et cerea regna refingunt.
saepe etiam duris errando in cotibus alas
attrivere ultroque animam sub fasce dedere:
tantus amor florum et generandi gloria mellis.   205
ergo ipsas quamvis angusti terminus aevi
excipiat, (neque enim plus septima ducitur aestas),
at genus immortale manet, multosque per annos
stat fortuna domus, et avi numerantur avorum.
praeterea regem non sic Aegyptus et ingens   210
Lydia nec populi Parthorum aut Medus Hydaspes
observant. rege incolumi mens omnibus una est;
amisso rupere fidem, constructaque mella
diripuere ipsae et cratis solvere favorum.
ille operum custos, illum admirantur et omnes   215
circumstant fremitu denso stipantque frequentes,
et saepe attollunt umeris et corpora bello
obiectant pulchramque petunt per vulnera mortem.

His quidam signis atque haec exempla secuti
esse apibus partem divinae mentis et haustus   220
aetherios dixere; deum namque ire per omnis
terrasque tractusque maris caelumque profundum;
hinc pecudes, armenta, viros, genus omne ferarum,
quemque sibi tenuis nascentem arcessere vitas:

Lax into love, nor bear with pangs of birth their young.
But all by themselves from leaves and sweet herbs they will
    gather   200
Their children in their mouths, keep up the queenly
    succession
And the birth-rate, restore the halls and the realm of wax.
Often, too, as they wander they bruise their wings on hard
Rocks, happy to die in harness beneath their burdens—
Such is their love for flowers, their pride in producing
    honey.   205
Though short their course of life, and death may catch
    them early,
(Seven summers they have at most),
The race remains immortal, for many years survive
The family fortunes, their fathers are known to the fourth
    generation.
Besides, they esteem royalty more than Egypt does or
    enormous   210
Lydia even, or the peoples of Parthia, or the Mede by
    Hydaspes.
Let the queen be safe—they are bound by a single faith
    and purpose:
Lose her—then unity's gone, and they loot the honey cells
They built themselves, and break down the honeycomb's
    withy wall.
Guardian of all their works she is. They hold her in awe.   215
Thick is their humming murmur as they crowd around her
    and mob her.
Often they chair her shoulder high: and in war they
    shelter
Her body with theirs, desiring the wounds of a noble death.
  Influenced by these signs and images, some have said
That bees partake of an Essence Divine and drink Heaven's
    well-springs,   220
For God (they hold) pervades
All lands, the widespread seas, the abysms of unplumbed
    sky:
From Whom flocks, herds, men, every wild creature in its
    kind
Derive at birth the slight, precarious breath of life:

scilicet huc reddi deinde ac resoluta referri   225
omnia, nec morti esse locum, sed viva volare
sideris in numerum atque alto succedere caelo.

 Si quando sedem augustam servataque mella
thesauri relines, prius haustu sparsus aquarum
ora fove, fumosque manu praetende sequacis.   230
bis gravidos cogunt fetus, duo tempora messis:—
Taygete simul os terris ostendit honestum
Pleas et Oceani spretos pede reppulit amnis,
aut eadem sidus fugiens ubi Piscis aquosi
tristior hibernas caelo descendit in undas.   235
illis ira modum supra est, laesaeque venenum
morsibus inspirant, et spicula caeca relinquunt
adfixae venis, animasque in vulnere ponunt.
sin duram metues hiemem parcesque futuro
contunsosque animos et res miserabere fractas,   240
at suffire thymo cerasque recidere inanis
quis dubitet? nam saepe favos ignotus adedit
stellio et lucifugis congesta cubilia blattis,
immunisque sedens aliena ad pabula fucus;
aut asper crabro imparibus se immiscuit armis,   245
aut dirum tiniae genus, aut invisa Minervae
laxos in foribus suspendit aranea cassis.
quo magis exhaustae fuerint, hoc acrius omnes
incumbent generis lapsi sarcire ruinas,
complebuntque foros et floribus horrea texent.   250

 Si vero, quoniam casus apibus quoque nostros
vita tulit, tristi languebunt corpora morbo—

To Him, therefore, all things return at last and in Him   225
Are re-absorbed—no room for death—and they soar to join
The stars' immortal muster, and reach the heights of heaven.
  If ever you wish to unseal the treasure-vaults of their
     palace
Where the honey's hoarded, first sprinkle yourself with water,
Rinse your mouth, and release a smoke to chivvy them
     out.   230
Twice a year men gather their harvest and heavy produce:—
As soon as Taÿgete the Pleiad has turned her handsome
Face to the earth and spurned with her foot the repulsed
     ocean;
Or again when, fleeing the star of the rainy Fish, she goes
Gloomily down the sky and is drowned in a winter sea.   235
Unbounded then is the rage of the bees, provoked they
     breathe
Venom into their stabs, they cling to your veins and bury
Their stings—oh yes, they put their whole souls into the
     wound.
But if you fear a hard winter for them and wish to provide
     for
The future, pitying their bruised spirits and bankrupt
     estate,   240
Even then you should trouble to fumigate with thyme
And cut back the empty cells. For often the newt unnoticed
Nibbles the combs, their cubicles are black with light-shun-
     ning beetles,
And the drone gate-crashes their dinner:
There's the assassin hornet who, heavier armed than
     they,   245
Mixes it: there's the sinister tribe of moths: and Minerva's
Bugbear, the spider, draping his slack nets over the doorway.
But the more exhausted the bees, the keener they'll be to
     mend
The wreck of their ruined state,
Re-stock the store-rooms and fashion the flowery gran-
     aries.   250
  Since life brings to the bees the same bad luck as to
     humans,
They may suffer severe illness—

quod iam non dubiis poteris cognoscere signis:
continuo est aegris alius color; horrida vultum
deformat macies; tum corpora luce carentum   255
exportant tectis et tristia funera ducunt:
aut illae pedibus conexae ad limina pendent,
aut intus clausis cunctantur in aedibus omnes
ignavaeque fame et contracto frigore pigrae.
tum sonus auditur gravior, tractimque susurrant,   260
frigidus ut quondam silvis immurmurat Auster,
ut mare sollicitum stridit refluentibus undis,
aestuat ut clausis rapidus fornacibus ignis.
hic iam galbaneos suadebo incendere odores
mellaque harundineis inferre canalibus, ultro   265
hortantem et fessas ad pabula nota vocantem.
proderit et tunsum gallae admiscere saporem
arentisque rosas, aut igni pinguia multo
defruta, vel psithia passos de vite racemos,
Cecropiumque thymum et grave olentia centaurea.   270
est etiam flos in pratis cui nomen amello
fecere agricolae, facilis quaerentibus herba;
namque uno ingentem tollit de caespite silvam,
aureus ipse, sed in foliis, quae plurima circum
funduntur, violae sublucet purpura nigrae;   275
saepe deum nexis ornatae torquibus arae;
asper in ore sapor; tonsis in vallibus illum
pastores et curva legunt prope flumina Mellae.
huius odorato radices incoque Baccho,
pabulaque in foribus plenis appone canistris.   280
    Sed si quem proles subito defecerit omnis,
nec genus unde novae stirpis revocetur habebit,
tempus et Arcadii memoranda inventa magistri
pandere, quoque modo caesis iam saepe iuvencis
insincerus apes tulerit cruor. altius omnem   285
expediam prima repetens ab origine famam.

An epidemic you'll know by certain definite signs.
The sick change colour at once, and their faces are deformed
By dreadful emaciation: the bodies of the dead   255
They carry out of doors and bear in a sad cortège:
With clutching feet they hang
From the doorway, or moon about within their closed
     mansion
Listless with hunger all, numbed by a cramping cold.
Then there is heard a deeper sound, a hum sustained   260
As when a chill south wind murmurs among woods
Or the waves of a troubled sea moan and hiss at the ebb-tide
Or fierce flames roar heaving behind a furnace door.
I recommend here that you burn the pungent galbanum,
And instil honey through pipes of reed, going out of your
     way   265
To coax the invalid creatures back to familiar food.
It's a good thing also to add the juice of pounded oak-apples,
And dried rose-leaves, or wine boiled rich over a strong fire,
Raisins from the Psythian vine,
Thyme of Attica, and centaury strong-smelling.   270
There's a flower of the meadow, too, that our farmers call
     'amellus':
It's easy enough to find,
For it raises up from a single stool a forest of stems;
Golden the disk, raying out into petals whose dark violet
Is shot with a purple shine: 275
Often the gods' altars are adorned with garlands of it:
Its taste is rough to the tongue: shepherds gather it on the
     close-cropped
Valley slopes and beside the meandering stream of Mella.
Boil the roots of this flower in fragrant wine, and serve it
In basketfuls at their door, a tonic food for the bees.   280
  But if a man's swarm shall suddenly fail him, so that he has
     no
Source for another brood,
It is time to detail the famous invention of an Arcadian
Bee-master, the process by which he often made
A culture of bees from the putrid blood of slaughtered
     bullocks.   285
I'll give you a full account, exploring the earliest sources.

nam qua Pellaei gens fortunata Canopi
accolit effuso stagnantem flumine Nilum
et circum pictis vehitur sua rura phaselis,
quaque pharetratae vicinia Persidis urget,   290
et diversa ruens septem discurrit in ora
usque coloratis amnis devexus ab Indis,
et viridem Aegyptum nigra fecundat harena,
omnis in hac certam regio iacit arte salutem.
exiguus primum atque ipsos contractus in usus   295
eligitur locus; hunc angustique imbrice tecti
parietibusque premunt artis: et quattuor addunt,
quattuor a ventis obliqua luce fenestras.
tum vitulus bima curvans iam cornua fronte
quaeritur; huic geminae nares et spiritus oris   300
multa reluctanti obstruitur, plagisque perempto
tunsa per integram solvuntur viscera pellem.
sic positum in clauso linquunt, et ramea costis
subiciunt fragmenta, thymum casiasque recentis.
hoc geritur Zephyris primum impellentibus undas,   305
ante novis rubeant quam prata coloribus, ante
garrula quam tignis nidum suspendat hirundo.
interea teneris tepefactus in ossibus umor
aestuat, et visenda modis animalia miris,
trunca pedum primo, mox et stridentia pennis,   310
miscentur, tenuemque magis magis aëra carpunt,
donec ut aestivis effusus nubibus imber
erupere, aut ut nervo pulsante sagittae,
prima leves ineunt si quando proelia Parthi.

Where the people of Macedonian Canopus, a lucky race,
Live by the wide and standing flood-waters of Nile, and go
The round of their own farmlands in little painted boats;
And where the boundaries of Persia, land of archers,
    approach,   290
And the river rolling down
Right from the dark Abyssinians makes a delta of seven
    mouths
And fertilizes green Egypt's fields with its black sludge—
All this region relies on the artifice I tell of.

First a small place is chosen, a site that is narrowed
    further   295
For this same purpose: they close it in with a pantile roof
And prisoning walls: they add
Four windows with slanting lights that face towards the
    four winds.
A two-year-old calf is obtained, whose horns are beginning
    to curve
From his forehead. They stopper up, though he struggle
    wildly, his two   300
Nostrils and breathing mouth, and they beat him to death
    with blows
That pound his flesh to pulp but leave the hide intact.
Battened down in that narrow room they leave him, under
    his ribs
Laying fresh cassia and thyme and broken branches.
This is done as soon as a west wind ruffles the water,   305
Before the meadows are flushed with vernal colour, before
The talkative martin hangs her nest under the rafters.
Meanwhile, within the marrowy bones of the calf, the
    humours
Grow warm, ferment, till appear creatures miraculous—
Limbless at first, but soon they fidget, their wings
    vibrate,   310
And more, more they sip, they drink the delicate air:
At last they come pouring out, like a shower from summer
    clouds,
Or thick and fast as arrows
When Parthian archers, their bowstrings throbbing, advance
    to battle.

Quis deus hanc, Musae, quis nobis extudit artem?   315
unde nova ingressus hominum experientia cepit?
pastor Aristaeus fugiens Peneia Tempe,
amissis, ut fama, apibus morboque fameque,
tristis ad extremi sacrum caput astitit amnis
multa querens, atque hac adfatus voce parentem: 320
'mater, Cyrene mater, quae gurgitis huius
ima tenes, quid me praeclara stirpe deorum
(si modo, quem perhibes, pater est Thymbraeus Apollo)
invisum fatis genuisti? aut quo tibi nostri
pulsus amor? quid me caelum sperare iubebas?   325
en etiam hunc ipsum vitae mortalis honorem,
quem mihi vix frugum et pecudum custodia sollers
omnia temptanti extuderat, te matre relinquo.
quin age et ipsa manu felicis erue silvas,
fer stabulis inimicum ignem atque interfice messis,   330
ure sata et validam in vitis molire bipennem,
tanta meae si te ceperunt taedia laudis.'
At mater sonitum thalamo sub fluminis alti
sensit. eam circum Milesia vellera Nymphae
carpebant hyali saturo fucata colore,   335
Drymoque Xanthoque Ligeaque Phyllodoceque,
caesariem effusae nitidam per candida colla,
Cydippeque et flava Lycorias, altera virgo,
altera tum primos Lucinae experta labores,
Clioque et Beroe soror, Oceanitides ambae,   340
ambae auro, pictis incinctae pellibus ambae,
atque Ephyre atque Opis et Asia Deiopea
et tandem positis velox Arethusa sagittis.
inter quas curam Clymene narrabat inanem

What god was it, my Muse, that worked this miracle for
    us?   315
Who caused this novel practice to cross the minds of men?
A shepherd called Aristaeus was leaving Thessalian Tempe,
His bees—so the story goes—destroyed by disease and famine;
And glum he stood by the hallowed river-head, invoking,
Upbraiding the one who bore him.   320
'O mother, my mother Cyrene, who dwell in the deep below
This pool, why did you bear me from the glorious seed of
    godhead
(If indeed, as you tell me, the god Apollo of Troas begat me)
To be fate's target? Where, where has your love for me flown?
Why tell me to hope for heaven?   325
Look, even this mere grace of mortal life, which I won
So hardly by craft and much resourcefulness from the care of
Harvest and herd—though you are my mother—I must
    abandon.
Go on, then, with your own hand grub up my happy
    orchards,
Be my enemy, set fire to my sheep-folds, murder the
    harvests,   330
Blast the sown fields, hack down the vines with a brutal axe,
If you find my praise so irksome.'
   His mother heard that cry from her room beneath the
    river.
The nymphs, her companions, were carding
Fleeces of Miletus dyed a rich glass-green colour—   335
Drymo, Xantho, Ligea, Phyllodoce were their names
And their tresses were loose and glittering about their snow-
    shine necks:
Cydippe too and corn-blonde Lycorias, one a virgin,
The other but now had felt her travail pains for the first
    time:
Clio and Beroe her sister, both Ocean princesses,   340
Both of them gold-adorned and girt with dappled skins:
The Ephyrean was there, and Opis, and Deiopeia,
And Arethusa the fleetfoot, her arrows at last laid by.
Clymene was telling the story of Vulcan, the trouble he
    took

Volcani, Martisque dolos et dulcia furta,   345
aque Chao densos divum numerabat amores.
carmine quo captae dum fusis mollia pensa
devolvunt, iterum maternas impulit auris
luctus Aristaei, vitreisque sedilibus omnes
obstipuere; sed ante alias Arethusa sorores   350
prospiciens summa flavum caput extulit unda,
et procul: 'o gemitu non frustra exterrita tanto,
Cyrene soror, ipse tibi, tua maxima cura,
tristis Aristaeus Penei genitoris ad undam
stat lacrimans, et te crudelem nomine dicit.'   355
huic percussa nova mentem formidine mater
'duc, age, duc ad nos; fas illi limina divum
tangere' ait. simul alta iubet discedere late
flumina, qua iuvenis gressus inferret. at illum
curvata in montis faciem circumstetit unda,   360
accepitque sinu vasto misitque sub amnem.
iamque domum mirans genetricis et umida regna
speluncisque lacus clausos lucosque sonantis
ibat, et ingenti motu stupefactus aquarum
omnia sub magna labentia flumina terra   365
spectabat diversa locis, Phasimque Lycumque,
et caput unde altus primus se erumpit Enipeus,
unde pater Tiberinus et unde Aniena fluenta,
saxosusque sonans Hypanis Mysusque Caicus,
et gemina auratus taurino cornua vultu   370
Eridanus, quo non alius per pinguia culta
in mare purpureum violentior effluit amnis.
postquam est in thalami pendentia pumice tecta
perventum et nati fletus cognovit inanis
Cyrene, manibus liquidos dant ordine fontis   375
germanae tonsisque ferunt mantelia villis;
pars epulis onerant mensas et plena reponunt

In vain, and how Mars tricked him and stole his sweet
    away,   345
Recounting the gods' continual amours from Chaos onwards.
While the nymphs were charmed by her song and the soft
    wool curled from their distaffs.
Once more his mother's ears
Thrilled to the shepherd's grief, and all of them on their
    glassy
Thrones were astounded: then, before the rest, Arethusa   350
Glanced forth, raising her golden head out of the pool,
And called from afar. 'You are right to be fluttered by such
    a wild
Lament, sister Cyrene, for he—your fondest care—
Aristaeus is weeping at the waterside of his father,
Naming you, calling you cruel.'   355
Then, heart frantic with fresh alarm, his mother said,
'Bring, oh bring him to me! No harm for him to approach
The gods' threshold.' At once she bade the stream roll back
And leave a wide path, an entrance for him. But the water
Stood up on end in a mountainous curve, stood all around
    him,   360
Laid him in its huge lap and bore him beneath the surface.
Marvelling now at his mother's home and aqueous kingdom—
The pools enclosed in caverns, the sighing woods of weed—
He went along: the enormous passage of waters dazed him,
For he viewed all the rivers that glide below great earth   365
Far and wide—Phasis, Lycus,
The spring from which the deep Enipeus first leaps forth,
The source of father Tiber and the flowing Anio,
Of Hypanis roaring down through rocks, Mysian Caicus,
Of Eridanus, depicted with gilded horns on his bull-
    head—   370
Eridanus, than which through fertile lands no river
Rushes with more momentum to the pansy-purple sea.
So he reached the overhanging roof of his mother's bower
Fashioned in porous stone, and she heard his fond lament.
Her sisters washed his hands   375
Duly with pure water and fetched the nappy towels:
Others loaded the table with a banquet and laid the
    brimming

pocula, Panchaeis adolescunt ignibus arae.
et mater 'cape Maeonii carchesia Bacchi:
Oceano libemus' ait. simul ipsa precatur   380
Oceanumque patrem rerum Nymphasque sorores,
centum quae silvas, centum quae flumina servant.
ter liquido ardentem perfundit nectare Vestam,
ter flamma ad summum tecti subiecta reluxit.
omine quo firmans animum sic incipit ipsa: 385
  'Est in Carpathio Neptuni gurgite vates,
caeruleus Proteus, magnum qui piscibus aequor
et iuncto bipedum curru metitur equorum.
hic nunc Emathiae portus patriamque revisit
Pallenen; hunc et Nymphae veneramur et ipse   390
grandaevus Nereus: novit namque omnia vates,
quae sint, quae fuerint, quae mox ventura trahantur;
quippe ita Neptuno visum est, immania cuius
armenta et turpis pascit sub gurgite phocas.
hic tibi, nate, prius vinclis capiendus, ut omnem   395
expediat morbi causam eventusque secundet.
nam sine vi non ulla dabit praecepta, neque illum
orando flectes; vim duram et vincula capto
tende; doli circum haec demum frangentur inanes.
ipsa ego te, medios cum sol accenderit aestus,   400
cum sitiunt herbae et pecori iam gratior umbra est,
in secreta senis ducam, quo fessus ab undis
se recipit, facile ut somno adgrediare iacentem.
verum ubi correptum manibus vinclisque tenebis,
tum variae eludent species atque ora ferarum.   405
fiet enim subito sus horridus atraque tigris
squamosusque draco et fulva cervice leaena,
aut acrem flammae sonitum dabit atque ita vinclis

Goblets, and fed the altar fire with Arabian incense.

Then his mother cried, 'Take up your cups of wine! Let
    us drink

A toast to Ocean!' Herself to Ocean at once she prayed, 380

Father of the universe, and the sisterhood of nymphs

Who are wardens over a hundred woods, a hundred rivers.

Three times did she pour on the hallowed hearth-fire the
    pure nectar,

Three times did the lowly flame leap up to ceiling height—

A sign that gave him heart. 385

    'There dwells in the Mediterranean a seer,' she began to
    say—

'Sea-blue Proteus, one who drives through the mighty deep

His chariot drawn by harnessed fish and two-legged horses.

He is visiting now the Macedonian ports and Pallene

His birth-place. Him we nymphs and ancient Nereus
    hold 390

In honour, for he knows all

That is, that has been, and all that is about to be—

Knows all by the god Neptune's grace, whose herds of
    monsters

And hideous seals he pastures in meadows submarine.

This seer, my son, you must bind in fetters before he'll tell
    you 395

The whole truth of your bees' sickness and put things right.

Except to violence he yields not one word of advice; entreaties

Have no effect: you must seize him, offer him force and
    fetters,

On which in the end his wiles will dash themselves to waste.

I myself, when the sun has flamed to full meridian, 400

When grass is thirsty and shade more grateful to the flocks,

Will lead you up to that ancient's den, where he withdraws

Tired from the waves, that easily you may attack him
    sleeping.

But when you have him fast in a handhold and fettered, then

With the guise and visage of various wild beasts he'll keep
    you guessing: 405

Suddenly he'll turn into a bristling boar, a black tiger,

A laminated dragon or lioness tawny-necked,

Or go up in a shrill burst of flame and thus from his fetters

excidet, aut in aquas tenuis dilapsus abibit.
sed quanto ille magis formas se vertet in omnis,   410
tam tu, nate, magis contende tenacia vincla,
donec talis erit mutato corpore, qualem
videris incepto tegeret cum lumina somno.'
    Haec ait et liquidum ambrosiae diffundit odorem,
quo totum nati corpus perfudit; at illi   415
dulcis compositis spiravit crinibus aura
atque habilis membris venit vigor. est specus ingens
exesi latere in montis, quo plurima vento
cogitur inque sinus scindit sese unda reductos,
deprensis olim statio tutissima nautis;   420
intus se vasti Proteus tegit obice saxi.
hic iuvenem in latebris aversum a lumine Nympha
conlocat, ipsa procul nebulis obscura resistit.
iam rabidus torrens sitientis Sirius Indos
ardebat caelo, et medium sol igneus orbem   425
hauserat; arebant herbae, et cava flumina siccis
faucibus ad limum radii tepefacta coquebant:
cum Proteus consueta petens e fluctibus antra
ibat; eum vasti circum gens umida ponti
exsultans rorem late dispergit amarum.   430
sternunt se somno diversae in litore phocae;
ipse, velut stabuli custos in montibus olim,
vesper ubi e pastu vitulos ad tecta reducit
auditisque lupos acuunt balatibus agni,
consedit scopulo medius, numerumque recenset.   435
cuius Aristaeo quoniam est oblata facultas,

Escape, or give you the slip gliding off in a trickle of water.

But the more he transforms himself, 410

The tighter, my son, you must strain the shackles that bind
his body,

Until at last it changes back to the first likeness

You saw at the start when his eyes were closing down in
sleep.'

Thus she spoke, and she sprayed a perfume of pure
ambrosia

Over her son's body, 415

So that his comely curls wafted a pleasing fragrance

And his limbs grew strong and lithe . . . There is a giant
cave

Hollowed out from the flank of a mountain where myriad
waves

Forced by the wind drive in and among its coves are
dispersed—

A cosy anchorage once for sailors caught in a storm. 420

Proteus shelters within behind a huge rock-barrier.

Here the nymph puts her son in a hiding-place out of the
light,

Standing herself at a distance, dim in the drapes of mist.

Now the raving Dog Star that burns parched Indians

Glared in the sky, and the fiery sun had finished half 425

His course: the grass was scorched: the river-beds, dry and
gasping,

Roasted in the sun's rays, were baked to a hot mud.

Now Proteus came to his customed

Den from the water: around him the dripping tribes of the
deep

Frolicked, flinging the bitter spray far and wide about
them. 430

All over the beach the seals were sprawled for their siesta.

The wizard himself, just like a herdsman might on the
mountains,

When evening herds the calves homeward out of their
pasture

And wolves prick up their ears hearing the lambs bleating,

Sat in the midst of them on a rock and took their tally. 435

Aristaeus saw his chance:

vix defessa senem passus componere membra
cum clamore ruit magno manicisque iacentem
occupat. ille suae contra non immemor artis
omnia transformat sese in miracula rerum,   440
ignemque horribilemque feram fluviumque liquentem.
verum ubi nulla fugam reperit fallacia, victus
in sese redit atque hominis tandem ore locutus:
'nam quis te, iuvenum confidentissime, nostras
iussit adire domos? quidve hinc petis?' inquit. at ille: 445
'scis, Proteu, scis ipse; neque est te fallere quicquam:
sed tu desine velle. deum praecepta secuti
venimus hinc lapsis quaesitum oracula rebus.'
tantum effatus. ad haec vates vi denique multa
ardentis oculos intorsit lumine glauco,   450
et graviter frendens sic fatis ora resolvit.—
    'Non te nullius exercent numinis irae;
magna luis commissa: tibi has miserabilis Orpheus
haudquaquam ob meritum poenas, ni fata resistant,
suscitat, et rapta graviter pro coniuge saevit.   455
illa quidem, dum te fugeret per flumina praeceps,
immanem ante pedes hydrum moritura puella
servantem ripas alta non vidit in herba.
at chorus aequalis Dryadum clamore supremos
implerunt montis; flerunt Rhodopeiae arces   460
altaque Pangaea et Rhesi Mavortia tellus
atque Getae atque Hebrus et Actias Orithyia.
ipse cava solans aegrum testudine amorem
te, dulcis coniunx, te solo in litore secum,
te veniente die, te decedente canebat.   465
Taenarias etiam fauces, alta ostia Ditis,

Scarcely letting the old man lay down his weary limbs,
He rushed him with a great shout and shackled him where he
  lay.
The wizard for his part remembered well his magic
And turned himself into all kinds of uncanny things— 440
Became a fire, a fearful wild beast, a flowing river.
But, seeing that no deception could spirit him away, beaten
He returned to himself and spoke at last in human tones.
'Boldest of youths, who bade you
Approach my house? What do you want with me?' The
  other,   445
'You know, Proteus, you know very well: for nothing escapes
  you.
Stop being stubborn. Obeying the gods' commands we are
  come
To ask the oracle how to revive my drooping fortunes.'
So much he said. At last now the seer convulsively
Rolled his glaring eyes so they shone with a glassy light, 450
Harshly ground his teeth, and thus gave tongue to Fate.—
 'Not without sanction divine is the anger that hunts you
  down
Great is the crime you pay for. Piteous Orpheus calls
This punishment on you. Well you deserve it. If destiny
So wills it. Bitter his anguish for the wife was taken from
  him.   455
Headlong beside that river she fled you. She never saw,
Poor girl, her death there, deep in the grass before her feet—
The watcher on the river-bank, the savage watersnake.
The band of wood-nymphs, her companions, filled with
  their crying
The hilltops: wailed the peaks of Rhodope: high
  Pangaea,   460
The unwarlike land of Rhesus,
The Getae lamented, and Hebrus, and Attic Orithyia.
Orpheus, sick to the heart, sought comfort of his hollow
  lyre:
You, sweet wife, he sang alone on the lonely shore,
You at the dawn of day he sang, at day's decline you. 465
The gorge of Taenarus even, deep gate of the Underworld,

et caligantem nigra formidine lucum
ingressus, manisque adiit regemque tremendum
nesciaque humanis precibus mansuescere corda.
at cantu commotae Erebi de sedibus imis   470
umbrae ibant tenues simulacraque luce carentum,
quam multa in foliis avium se milia condunt,
vesper ubi aut hibernus agit de montibus imber,
matres atque viri defunctaque corpora vita
magnanimum heroum, pueri innuptaeque puellae,   475
impositique rogis iuvenes ante ora parentum—
quos circum limus niger et deformis harundo
Cocyti tardaque palus inamabilis unda
alligat et novies Styx interfusa coercet.
quin ipsae stupuere domus atque intima Leti   480
Tartara caeruleosque implexae crinibus anguis
Eumenides, tenuitque inhians tria Cerberus ora;
atque Ixionii vento rota constitit orbis.
iamque pedem referens casus evaserat omnis,
redditaque Eurydice superas veniebat ad auras   485
pone sequens (namque hanc dederat Proserpina legem),
cum subita incautum dementia cepit amantem,
ignoscenda quidem, scirent si ignoscere manes:
restitit, Eurydicenque suam iam luce sub ipsa
immemor heu! victusque animi respexit. ibi omnis   490
effusus labor, atque immitis rupta tyranni
foedera, terque fragor stagnis auditus Averni.
illa 'quis et me,' inquit, 'miseram et te perdidit, Orpheu,
quis tantus furor? en iterum crudelia retro

He entered, and that grove where fear hangs like a black
    fog:
Approached the ghostly people, approached the King of
    Terrors
And the hearts that know not how to be touched by human
    prayer.
But, by his song aroused from Hell's nethermost base-
    ments,   470
Flocked out the flimsy shades, the phantoms lost to light,
In number like to the millions of birds that hide in the leaves
When evening or winter rain from the hills has driven them—
Mothers and men, the dead
Bodies of great-heart heroes, boys and unmarried
    maidens,   475
Young men laid on the pyre before their parents' eyes—
And about them lay the black ooze, the crooked reeds of
    Cocytus,
Bleak the marsh that barred them in with its stagnant water,
And the Styx coiling nine times around corralled them there.
Why, Death's very home and holy of holies was shaken   480
To hear that song, and the Furies with steel-blue snakes
    entwined
In their tresses; the watch-dog Cerberus gaped open his triple
    mouth;
Ixion's wheel stopped dead from whirling in the wind.
And now he's avoided every pitfall of the homeward path,
And Eurydice, regained, is nearing the upper air   485
Close behind him (for this condition has Proserpine made),
When a moment's madness catches her lover off his guard—
Pardonable, you'd say, but Death can never pardon.
He halts. Eurydice, his own, is now on the lip of
Daylight. Alas! he forgot. His purpose broke. He looked
    back.   490
His labour was lost, the pact he had made with the merciless
    king
Annulled. Three times did thunder peal over the pools of
    Avernus.
"Who," she cried, "has doomed me to misery, who has
    doomed us?
What madness beyond measure? Once more a cruel fate

fata vocant, conditque natantia lumina somnus.   495
iamque vale: feror ingenti circumdata nocte
invalidasque tibi tendens, heu non tua, palmas.'
dixit et ex oculis subito, ceu fumus in auras
commixtus tenuis, fugit diversa, neque illum
prensantem nequiquam umbras et multa volentem   500
dicere praeterea vidit; nec portitor Orci
amplius obiectam passus transire paludem.
    quid faceret? quo se rapta bis coniuge ferret?
quo fletu manis, quae numina voce moveret?
illa quidem Stygia nabat iam frigida cumba.   505
septem illum totos perhibent ex ordine mensis
rupe sub aëria deserti ad Strymonis undam
flevisse et gelidis haec evolvisse sub astris
mulcentem tigris et agentem carmine quercus;
qualis populea maerens philomela sub umbra   510
amissos queritur fetus, quos durus arator
observans nido implumis detraxit; at illa
flet noctem, ramoque sedens miserabile carmen
integrat, et maestis late loca questibus implet.
nulla Venus, non ulli animum flexere hymenaei: 515
solus Hyperboreas glacies Tanaimque nivalem
arvaque Riphaeis numquam viduata pruinis
lustrabat, raptam Eurydicen atque inrita Ditis
dona querens. spretae Ciconum quo munere matres
inter sacra deum nocturnique orgia Bacchi   520
discerptum latos iuvenem sparsere per agros.
tum quoque marmorea caput a cervice revulsum

Drags me away, and my swimming eyes are drowned in
   darkness.   495
Good-bye. I am borne away. A limitless night is about me
And over the strengthless hands I stretch to you, yours no
   longer."
Thus she spoke: and at once from his sight, like a wisp of
   smoke
Thinned into air, was gone.
Wildly he grasped at shadows, wanting to say much
   more,   500
But she did not see him; nor would the ferryman of the
   Inferno
Let him again cross the fen that lay between them.
   What could he do, where go, his wife twice taken from
   him?
What lament would move Death now? What deities hear his
   song?
Cold she was voyaging now over the Stygian stream.   505
Month after month, they say, for seven months alone
He wept beneath a crag high up by the lonely waters
Of Strymon, and under the ice-cold stars poured out his
   dirge
That charmed the tigers and made the oak trees follow him.
As a nightingale he sang that sorrowing under a poplar's   510
Shade laments the young she has lost, whom a heartless
   ploughman
Has noticed and dragged from the nest unfledged; and the
   nightingale
Weeps all night, on a branch repeating the piteous song,
Loading the acres around with the burden of her lament.
No love, no marriage could turn his mind away from
   grief: 515
Alone through Arctic ice, through the snows of Tanais, over
Frost-bound Riphaean plateaux
He ranged, bewailing his lost Eurydice and the wasted
Bounty of Death. In the end Thracian Bacchantes, flouted
By his neglect, one night in the midst of their Master's
   revels   520
Tore him limb from limb and scattered him over the land.
But even then that head, plucked from the marble-pale

gurgite cum medio portans Oeagrius Hebrus
volveret, Eurydicen vox ipsa et frigida lingua
a miseram Eurydicen! anima fugiente vocabat,   525
Eurydicen toto referebant flumine ripae.'
    Haec Proteus, et se iactu dedit aequor in altum,
quaque dedit, spumantem undam sub vertice torsit.
    At non Cyrene; namque ultro adfata timentem:
'nate, licet tristis animo deponere curas.   530
haec omnis morbi causa, hinc miserabile Nymphae,
cum quibus illa choros lucis agitabat in altis,
exitium misere apibus. tu munera supplex
tende petens pacem, et facilis venerare Napaeas;
namque dabunt veniam votis, irasque remittent.   535
sed modus orandi qui sit prius ordine dicam.
quattuor eximios praestanti corpore tauros,
qui tibi nunc viridis depascunt summa Lycaei,
delige, et intacta totidem cervice iuvencas.
quattuor his aras alta ad delubra dearum   540
constitue, et sacrum iugulis demitte cruorem,
corporaque ipsa boum frondoso desere luco.
post, ubi nona suos Aurora ostenderit ortus,
inferias Orphei Lethaea papavera mittes
et nigram mactabis ovem, lucumque revises,   545
placatam Eurydicen vitula venerabere caesa.'
    Haud mora: continuo matris praecepta facessit;
ad delubra venit, monstratas excitat aras,
quattuor eximios praestanti corpore tauros
ducit et intacta totidem cervice iuvencas.   550
post, ubi nona suos Aurora induxerat ortus,
inferias Orphei mittit lucumque revisit.
hic vero subitum ac dictu mirabile monstrum
aspiciunt, liquefacta boum per viscera toto

Neck, and rolling down mid-stream on the river Hebrus—
That voice, that cold, cold tongue cried out "Eurydice!"
Cried "Poor Eurydice!" as the soul of the singer fled,   525
And the banks of the river echoed, echoed "Eurydice!" '
    Thus Proteus spake, and dived into the sea's depths,
And where he dived the water, foaming, spun in a funnel.
    Cyrene waited and spoke a word to her frightened son:
'You may cast your cares away,'   530
She said, 'for here is the whole truth of your bees' sickness
And the death they were dealt by the nymphs with whom
    Eurydice
Danced in the deep woods. So offer them gifts and make
    your
Peace with them, and pray to the Gracious Ones of the
    grove.
They will answer your prayers with forgiveness, they will
    forget their anger.   535
But first let me tell you the form your orisons must take.
Choose four bulls of excellent body that now on the heights
    of
Green Lycaeus are grazing,
And as many heifers whose necks have never felt the yoke.
Build for these four altars beside the lofty shrines   540
Of the goddesses, and let the sacred blood from their throats,
Then leave the oxen's bodies alone in a leafy thicket.
When the ninth day has dawned
You shall send oblivion's poppies as a funeral gift to Orpheus,
Slay a calf in honour of Eurydice placated,   545
Slaughter a black ewe and go to the thicket again.'
    Without delay he acts at once on his mother's advice:
He comes to the shrine, erects—as she told him—altars, and
    brings
Four bulls of excellent body
With as many heifers whose necks have never felt the
    yoke: 550
When the ninth day has dawned,
Sends funeral gifts to Orpheus and goes to the thicket again.
Here, to be sure, a miracle sudden and strange to tell of
They behold: from the oxen's bellies all over their rotting
    flesh

stridere apes utero et ruptis effervere costis, 555
immensasque trahi nubes, iamque arbore summa
confluere et lentis uvam demittere ramis.

Haec super arvorum cultu pecorumque canebam
et super arboribus, Caesar dum magnus ad altum
fulminat Euphraten bello victorque volentis 560
per populos dat iura viamque adfectat Olympo.
illo Vergilium me tempore dulcis alebat
Parthenope, studiis florentem ignobilis oti,
carmina qui lusi pastorum audaxque iuventa,
Tityre, te patulae cecini sub tegmine fagi. 565

Creatures are humming, swarming through the wreckage of
    their ribs—   555
Huge and trailing clouds of bees, that now in the treetops
Unite and hang like a bunch of grapes from the pliant
    branches.

    Thus of agriculture and the care of flocks I sang
And forestry, while great Caesar fired his lightnings and
    conquered
By deep Euphrates, and gave justice to docile peoples,   560
Winning his way to the Immortals.
This was the time when I, Virgil, nurtured in sweetest
Parthenope, did follow unknown to fame the pursuits
Of peace, who dallied with pastoral verse, and by youth
    emboldened,
Tityrus, sang of you in the shade of a spreading beech.   565